The Ultimate
Crock Pot

Cookbook for Beginners

2000+ Days of Effortless and Tasty Slow Cooker Recipes | Crockpot Recipe Book to Unleash the Cooking Master in You

Mariela Lemley

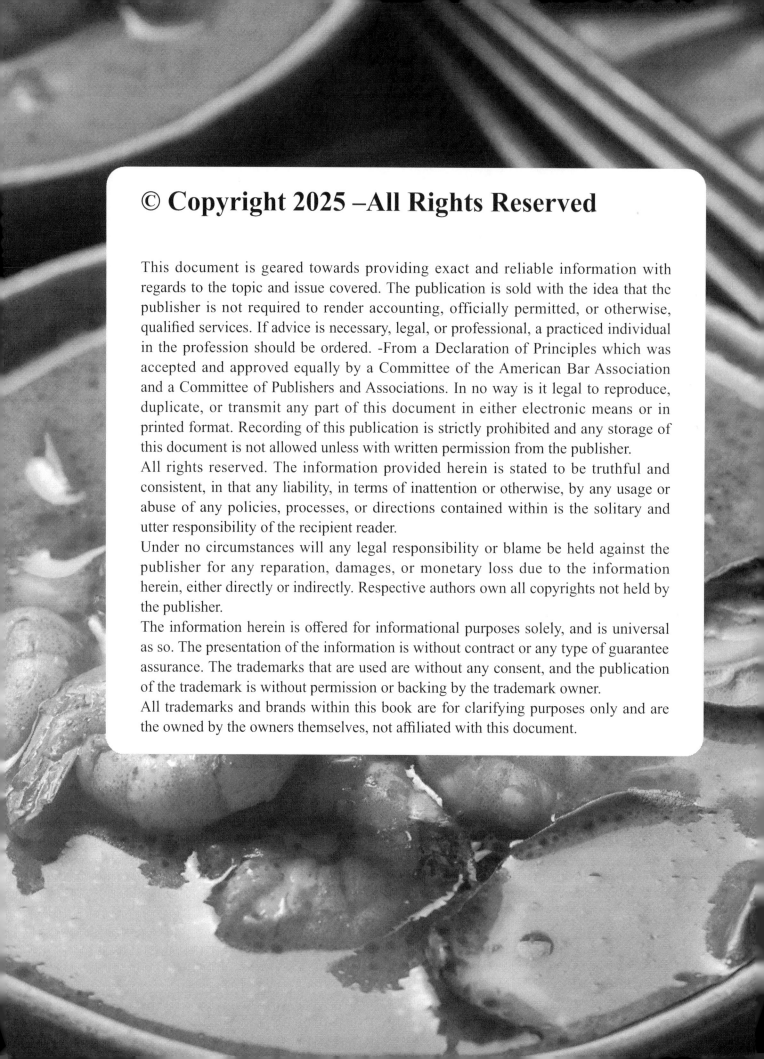

Table of Contents

Introduction

The crock pot, often referred to as a slow cooker, is a game-changer in the culinary world, designed to make home cooking effortless and enjoyable. Its ingenious "set it and forget it" functionality has transformed meal preparation, allowing busy individuals and families to enjoy wholesome, flavorful dishes with minimal effort. Whether you're a novice cook or an experienced chef, the crock pot offers an unparalleled level of convenience without compromising on taste or quality.

At its heart, the crock pot is a simple yet effective appliance. By cooking food slowly at a consistent temperature, it breaks down ingredients gently, enhancing their natural flavors and textures. This method not only delivers tender meats and rich sauces but also locks in nutrients, making meals healthier and more satisfying. From hearty stews and savory casseroles to comforting soups and even decadent desserts, the crock pot handles it all with ease.

The appeal of the crock pot extends beyond its culinary capabilities. Its time-saving nature allows you to prepare meals in advance, letting you focus on your day while it does the work. Simply add your ingredients, adjust the settings, and return to a perfectly cooked meal. This makes it ideal for busy professionals, families juggling hectic schedules, or anyone who wants to streamline their cooking routine.

In addition to its practicality, the crock pot is a versatile tool that adapts to a variety of cuisines and cooking styles. From slow-cooked Italian pastas to spicy curries and classic pot roasts, the possibilities are endless. Its ability to cater to different dietary needs—whether vegetarian, low-carb, or gluten-free—makes it a universally loved appliance.

The crock pot isn't just an appliance; it's a companion in the kitchen that encourages creativity and enhances the joy of cooking. With its ability to deliver flavor-packed meals that bring people together, the crock pot has earned its place as an indispensable tool for modern households. Whether you're hosting a dinner party or preparing a quiet meal for your family, the crock pot ensures every dish is a success.

Fundamentals of the Crock Pot

The crock pot, commonly known as a slow cooker, is a countertop kitchen appliance designed to cook food at low, consistent temperatures over an extended period. It's an essential tool for busy households, offering the convenience of preparing meals in advance. The crock pot works by enclosing heat within a ceramic or metal pot, allowing ingredients to simmer gently. This method enhances flavors and tenderizes ingredients, creating rich, hearty dishes. From soups and stews to roasts and desserts, the crock pot is incredibly versatile. Its energy-efficient design and hands-free operation make it ideal for preparing meals while you focus on other tasks. Additionally, the slow cooking process helps retain nutrients, making meals healthier. Whether you're an experienced chef or a beginner, the crock pot simplifies cooking without compromising taste or quality.

What Is the Crock Pot?

Crock pot is a versatile and user-friendly kitchen appliance that has become a staple in modern households. Designed to cook meals slowly at a low, steady temperature, the crock pot allows you to create flavorful, wholesome dishes with minimal effort. Its design typically includes a ceramic or metal pot encased in a heating element, topped with a secure lid to retain heat and moisture.

What makes the crock pot unique is its ability to cook meals over several hours, breaking down ingredients to enhance their natural flavors. This makes it perfect for dishes like stews, soups, casseroles, and even desserts. Meats become tender, vegetables develop deeper flavors, and sauces thicken beautifully—all without constant supervision.

One of the primary advantages of using a crock pot is its convenience. Simply prepare your ingredients, set the desired temperature and cooking time, and let the appliance do the rest. It's ideal for busy individuals or families, allowing you to prepare meals ahead of time and return home to a warm, ready-to-serve dinner. The crock pot's energy efficiency is another plus, as it consumes less power compared to traditional ovens.

Beyond practicality, the crock pot is versatile enough to cater to a range of dietary preferences and cuisines. From vegan dishes to hearty meat-based meals, the crock pot accommodates various cooking styles. Its ability to handle everything from slow-cooked curries to baked bread and even cakes makes it a must-have kitchen tool.

The crock pot is more than an appliance—it's a solution for stress-free cooking and a gateway to delicious, home-cooked meals. Whether for weeknight dinners or special occasions, the crock pot delivers convenience, flavor, and satisfaction.

Types of Crock Pots

Crock Pots, also known as slow cookers, come in a variety of types to suit different cooking needs, lifestyles, and preferences. Understanding the types available can help you choose the perfect one for your kitchen.

Basic Manual Crock Pots

These are the simplest and most affordable Crock Pots, featuring manual dials to control heat settings (low, high, and sometimes warm). They are ideal for straightforward recipes and are easy to use, making them great for beginners. However, they require manual operation and don't have advanced features like timers or digital controls.

Programmable Crock Pots

Programmable Crock Pots offer more flexibility and control. Equipped with digital displays and timers, these models allow you to set specific cooking times and temperatures. Once the cooking time is complete, they often switch to a "keep warm" mode automatically. These are ideal for busy individuals who want to set it and forget it.

Multi-Cookers

Some Crock Pots come with additional functionalities, such as sautéing, steaming, or pressure cooking. These versatile appliances are perfect for those who want to consolidate multiple cooking tools into one. While slightly more expensive, they save counter space and expand your culinary possibilities.

Travel-Friendly Crock Pots

Designed with portability in mind, these models come with locking lids and carrying handles, making them perfect for potlucks, parties, or family gatherings. They help prevent spills and keep food warm during transport.

Mini Crock Pots

Compact in size, mini Crock Pots are perfect for single servings, side dishes, or dips. They are ideal for small households, dorms, or those with limited kitchen space.

Split-Pot Crock Pots

These models feature dual compartments, allowing you to cook two different dishes simultaneously. Perfect for entertaining or preparing multiple dishes for a meal, these Crock Pots offer added convenience.

With a variety of options available, there's a Crock Pot to suit every need, whether you're cooking for one, feeding a family, or hosting a gathering.

Benefits of Using It

The crock pot, or slow cooker, has become a trusted kitchen companion for its ability to simplify meal preparation and deliver delicious results. Its benefits go beyond convenience, offering a host of advantages for cooks of all experience levels.

1. Time-Saving Convenience

One of the most significant advantages of the crock pot is its hands-free operation. Simply prepare your ingredients, place them in the pot, set the cooking time and temperature, and let it work its magic. This allows you to focus on other tasks, whether at home or away, while your meal cooks to perfection. It's an ideal solution for busy households, ensuring dinner is ready without last-minute stress.

2. Enhanced Flavor Development

The slow cooking process allows ingredients to simmer gently, melding flavors and creating deeply satisfying dishes. Meats become tender and juicy, vegetables take on rich, robust flavors, and sauces thicken beautifully. Whether you're making a hearty stew or a flavorful curry, the crock pot elevates the taste of every dish.

3. Nutrient Retention

Unlike high-heat cooking methods that can strip ingredients of essential nutrients, the crock pot's low and slow cooking preserves vitamins and minerals. This makes it an excellent choice for preparing nutrient-dense meals, especially when cooking fresh vegetables and lean proteins.

4. Cost Efficiency

The crock pot's energy consumption is minimal compared to traditional ovens or stovetops, making it a budget-friendly option. Additionally, it excels at making the most of affordable ingredients. Tougher cuts of meat, which are often less expensive, become tender and flavorful after slow cooking, offering gourmet results at a fraction of the cost.

5. Versatility in Cooking

From soups, stews, and roasts to desserts and even beverages, the crock pot can handle a wide variety of recipes. Its versatility allows you to explore different cuisines and cooking styles, accommodating everything from comforting classics to adventurous dishes. You can even bake bread or prepare yogurt in some models.

6. Meal Prep and Batch Cooking

The crock pot's large capacity makes it perfect for batch cooking. Prepare large quantities of soups, chili, or casseroles to portion and freeze for future meals. This approach not only saves time but also ensures you always have homemade meals ready when needed.

7. Ease of Cleaning

With most crock pots featuring removable, dishwasher-safe inserts, cleaning up is effortless. The minimal use of pots and pans further reduces post-meal chores, making the crock pot a practical choice for busy lifestyles.

8. Stress-Free Entertaining

Hosting a gathering? The crock pot allows you to prepare crowd-pleasing dishes in advance, freeing you to focus on your guests. From dips and appetizers to hearty mains, it simplifies entertaining while keeping food warm for hours.

The crock pot is more than just a kitchen gadget—it's a lifestyle enhancer. Its convenience, efficiency, and ability to create flavorful, wholesome meals make it a must-have for anyone seeking to simplify their cooking routine without compromising quality.

Before First Use

Preparing your crock pot for its first use ensures optimal performance and safe cooking. Follow these steps to get started:

Unpack and Inspect

Carefully remove the crock pot and its components from the packaging. Ensure all parts, including the lid, stoneware insert, and base, are present and in good condition. Discard any plastic or foam packaging materials.

Read the Manual

Take time to read the included user manual. Familiarize yourself with the operating instructions, safety precautions, and maintenance tips specific to your crock pot model.

Clean All Components

Wash the removable stoneware insert and glass lid in warm, soapy water. Rinse thoroughly and dry with a soft cloth. If your model includes any additional accessories, clean them as well. Never immerse the electrical base in water; instead, wipe it with a damp cloth and dry immediately.

Check for Placement

Place your crock pot on a flat, heat-resistant surface with adequate ventilation. Ensure it's positioned away from walls, appliances, or flammable materials. Leave at least 6 inches of space around the unit for proper airflow.

Perform a Test Run

Before cooking your first meal, run the crock pot on its lowest setting with water in the stoneware insert. This helps eliminate any residual manufacturing odors and ensures the unit functions correctly.

Prepare for Your First Recipe

Once cleaned and tested, your crock pot is ready to create delicious, slow-cooked meals. Begin with a simple recipe to familiarize yourself with its cooking settings and timing.

By following these steps, you'll set your crock pot up for safe and efficient use, ensuring countless enjoyable meals ahead.

How to Use the Crock Pot?

Using a crock pot is simple and convenient, making it a favorite for preparing hearty, slow-cooked meals. Follow these steps for the best results:

Prepare Your Ingredients
Chop, dice, or season your ingredients as required by your recipe. To ensure even cooking, cut vegetables and proteins into uniform sizes. For recipes requiring browned meats, sear them in a separate pan before adding them to the crock pot for added flavor.

Assemble the Crock Pot
Place the stoneware insert into the base of the crock pot. Add your ingredients in layers, starting with the denser ones, like root vegetables, at the bottom.

Select a Setting
Plug in your crock pot and choose the desired heat setting—typically low, high, or warm. Low heat is ideal for slow cooking over 6–10 hours, while high heat cooks meals faster in 4–6 hours. The warm setting keeps food ready for serving without overcooking.

Cover and Cook
Place the lid securely on the crock pot to trap heat and moisture. Avoid lifting the lid during cooking, as this releases heat and extends cooking time.

Check for Doneness
Near the end of the cooking time, use a meat thermometer to check the internal temperature of meats or test the texture of vegetables to ensure they're properly cooked.

Serve and Enjoy
Turn off the crock pot, carefully remove the stoneware insert, and serve your meal. For easy cleaning, allow the crock pot to cool completely before washing.

Tips and Tricks for Using the Crock Pot

Plan Ahead
Prep ingredients the night before to streamline your cooking process. Store prepped items in the refrigerator and assemble them in the crock pot the next morning.

Layer Wisely
Place denser ingredients, like carrots and potatoes, at the bottom. Lighter items, such as leafy greens or pasta, should go on top to prevent overcooking.

Don't Overfill
Avoid filling the crock pot beyond two-thirds of its capacity. Overfilling can lead to uneven cooking and spillovers.

Use the Right Liquids
Only a small amount of liquid is required, as the sealed lid prevents evaporation. Too much liquid can dilute flavors and alter the texture of your dish.

Resist Lifting the Lid
Each time you lift the lid, heat escapes, and cooking time increases. Only remove the lid when absolutely necessary, especially in the first few hours.

Customize Recipes
Traditional recipes can be adapted for the crock pot. Reduce liquids by about one-third, as they don't evaporate like they would in oven or stovetop cooking.

Utilize the Warm Setting
Use the warm setting to keep meals ready for serving after the cooking time ends. It prevents overcooking while keeping the dish at a safe serving temperature.

Clean Immediately
Soak the stoneware insert and lid in warm, soapy water immediately after use. This makes

cleaning easier and prevents food from sticking.

With these tips, your crock pot will become an indispensable tool for creating effortless, flavorful meals!

What Kind of Food Can I Make in My Crock Pot?

Crock pot is a versatile kitchen appliance that allows you to prepare a wide range of dishes effortlessly. Whether you're a fan of hearty comfort foods, light meals, or indulgent desserts, the crock pot can do it all. Here are some ideas for the types of food you can make:

1. Soups and Stews

One of the most popular uses for a crock pot is making soups and stews. From classic chicken noodle soup to hearty beef stew or creamy tomato bisque, the slow cooking process helps meld flavors beautifully. Toss in vegetables, meat, and broth, and let the crock pot do the rest.

2. Casseroles

Crock pots are perfect for preparing casseroles. Dishes like cheesy broccoli and rice casserole or lasagna come together effortlessly. Layer your ingredients, set the timer, and you'll have a warm, comforting meal without the need to use an oven.

3. Roast Meats

Whether it's beef, pork, or chicken, crock pots excel at producing tender, juicy roasts. Add vegetables and a flavorful marinade or broth for a complete meal. Pulled pork, pot roast, and whole roasted chicken are some favorites that turn out perfectly in a crock pot.

4. Pasta and Rice Dishes

Dishes like spaghetti bolognese, macaroni and cheese, or jambalaya can be made with ease in a crock pot. The low, consistent heat ensures the starches absorb flavors while cooking evenly.

5. Vegetarian Meals

From lentil curries to stuffed bell peppers, crock pots can create a variety of meat-free dishes. The long cooking time enhances the natural flavors of vegetables and legumes.

6. Breakfast Dishes

Start your day with minimal effort by preparing oatmeal, breakfast casseroles, or even frittatas in your crock pot overnight. Wake up to a warm, ready-to-eat breakfast.

7. Desserts

Crock pots can handle sweets, too! Prepare puddings, cobblers, cheesecakes, or even molten chocolate lava cakes with ease. The steady heat ensures even cooking without burning.

8. Sauces and Dips

Make homemade sauces like marinara, barbecue, or even apple butter. For gatherings, prepare warm, gooey dips such as spinach artichoke dip or queso.

9. Beans and Legumes

Perfectly cook beans, chickpeas, or lentils without soaking. Use them for soups, salads, or side dishes.

10. Drinks

Warm beverages like mulled cider, hot chocolate, or spiced wine can be easily prepared and kept warm for serving in a crock pot.

With its flexibility and ease of use, a crock pot can help you create an endless array of dishes, making it a must-have for any kitchen.

Clean and Maintenance for the Crock Pot

Proper cleaning and maintenance of your crock pot will ensure its longevity and keep it functioning efficiently. Follow these steps to keep your crock pot in top condition:

Cleaning After Each Use

Unplug and Cool

Always unplug the crock pot and let it cool completely before cleaning. Cleaning a hot unit can lead to damage or injury.

Remove the Stoneware Insert

Carefully lift the stoneware insert and lid from the base. These are the parts that come into direct contact with food and will require the most cleaning.

Soak and Wash

Place the stoneware insert and lid in warm, soapy water. Let them soak for a few minutes to loosen any stuck-on food. Use a non-abrasive sponge or cloth to gently scrub the surface. For stubborn stains, a paste of baking soda and water can be used as a mild abrasive.

Rinse Thoroughly

Rinse both the stoneware and lid with clean water to remove all soap residue. Dry them with a soft towel or allow them to air dry.

Wipe the Base

The base, which houses the heating element, should never be submerged in water. Instead, wipe it clean with a damp cloth. Use a gentle cleaner if needed but avoid abrasive materials that can scratch the surface.

Deep Cleaning

Tackle Stains and Odors
If your stoneware develops stains or retains odors, fill it with a mixture of water and white vinegar (equal parts) and let it sit for an hour. Rinse thoroughly afterward.

Clean Burnt-On Food
For stubborn, burnt-on food, fill the stoneware insert with warm water and a small amount of dish soap. Let it soak overnight, then scrub gently.

Maintenance Tips

Inspect Regularly
Periodically check the power cord and base for signs of wear or damage. If you notice any issues, discontinue use and contact the manufacturer.

Store Properly
Ensure all parts are completely dry before storing. Store the stoneware insert and lid separately or stack them carefully to prevent chipping or cracking.

Avoid Abrasives
Never use steel wool or harsh chemicals on your crock pot, as these can damage the surface.

Prevent Overflows
Avoid overfilling the crock pot during use, as spills can seep into the base and damage the heating element.

By following these steps, your crock pot will remain a reliable kitchen companion for years to come, delivering delicious and hassle-free meals.

Frequently Asked Questions & Notes

Frequently Asked Questions

Can I leave the crock pot on while I'm away from home?
Yes, crock pots are designed to cook safely for extended periods. Just ensure it's on a flat surface, away from flammable items, and set to the appropriate heat level.

Do I need to stir the food while it's cooking?
No, stirring is usually unnecessary, as the crock pot's design ensures even cooking. Stir only if the recipe specifically requires it.

Can I put frozen meat or vegetables directly into the crock pot?
It's recommended to thaw ingredients first to ensure even cooking and food safety. Using frozen items may result in uneven cooking.

Are the crock pot's stoneware insert and lid dishwasher-safe?
Yes, most stoneware inserts and glass lids are dishwasher-safe. Always refer to the manufacturer's instructions for specific care recommendations.

What liquids should I use in the crock pot?
You can use broth, water, or sauces, but ensure there's enough liquid to prevent burning. Avoid using too little, as it may affect the cooking process.

Can I cook on the high setting the entire time?
You can, but the low setting is better for recipes requiring slow, gentle cooking, as it develops deeper flavors and tenderness.

How do I prevent my food from sticking to the pot?
Apply a light coating of cooking spray or oil to the stoneware before adding ingredients. Alternatively, use crock pot liners for easier cleanup.

Why does the lid collect condensation?
This is normal. The condensation helps keep the food moist, as the crock pot operates in a sealed environment.

Can I reheat food in the crock pot?
It's not recommended to use the crock pot solely for reheating. Instead, reheat food in a microwave or stovetop, then use the crock pot to keep it warm.

Why is my food overcooked or dry?
Overcooking can happen if the recipe's cooking time isn't followed or if there's insufficient liquid. Always use the correct settings and monitor liquid levels.

Notes
Always check the manufacturer's guidelines for specific care instructions.

Avoid using metal utensils to prevent scratching the stoneware.

Ensure proper storage of leftovers by transferring them to a separate container before refrigerating.

4-Week Meal Plan

Week 1

Day 1:
Breakfast: Coconut Bacon and Eggs Breakfast Casserole
Lunch: Classic Barley and Chickpea Risotto
Dinner: Tender Spiced Turkey Breast
Dessert: Sweet Ginger Poached Pears

Day 2:
Breakfast: Deep-Dish Cheese Cauliflower Crust Breakfast Pizza
Lunch: Healthy Vegan Jambalaya
Dinner: Flavorful Italian Pork with Beans and Greens
Dessert: Summer Blueberry Slump with Dumplings

Day 3:
Breakfast: Healthy Keto Granola
Lunch: Simple Spaghetti Squash
Dinner: Easy All-In-One Lamb-Vegetable Dinner
Dessert: Walnut Banana Bread

Day 4:
Breakfast: Creamy Overnight Pumpkin Pie
Lunch: Fresh Corn On the Cob
Dinner: Tender Beef Stew
Dessert: Lucky Chai Tapioca Pudding

Day 5:
Breakfast: Cheesy Sausage & Egg Stuffed Mushrooms
Lunch: Fiber-Rich Potato and Corn Chowder
Dinner: Sweet and Sour Scallops with Pineapples
Dessert: Winter Warm Gingerbread

Day 6:
Breakfast: Easy Spinach Quiche
Lunch: Delicious Ratatouille
Dinner: Easy Juicy "Roasted" Duck
Dessert: Basic Almond Golden Cake

Day 7:
Breakfast: Classic Cheese Soufflé
Lunch: Basil Roasted Peppers
Dinner: Cheesy Steak Roulades with Spinach & Olives
Dessert: Hearty Pumpkin Pie Oats

Week 2

Day 1:
Breakfast: Sweet Apple Cherry Granola Crisp
Lunch: Nutritious Sweet-Braised Red Cabbage
Dinner: Italian Turkey Meatloaf with Baked Potatoes
Dessert: Walnut Banana Bread

Day 2:
Breakfast: Authentic Shakshuka
Lunch: Homemade Rosemary-Maple Beets
Dinner: Rosemary Lamb Shanks with Wild Mushroom
Dessert: Homemade Strawberry Cobbler

Day 3:
Breakfast: Hash Brown and Sausage Casserole
Lunch: Tasty North African Vegetable Stew
Dinner: BBQ Pulled Pork Sliders
Dessert: Chocolate Chip Brownies

Day 4:
Breakfast: Matzonhs Spinach Pie
Lunch: Traditional Ratatouille
Dinner: Juicy Creamy Chicken Stew
Dessert: Traditional Winter Gingerbread

Day 5:
Breakfast: Fresh Pear, Apple, and Cranberry Pancake Topping
Lunch: Cheesy Balsamic Brussels Sprouts with Pine Nuts
Dinner: Juicy Beef Steak and Veggies
Dessert: Holiday Chocolate-Covered Nut Clusters

Day 6:
Breakfast: Savory Tex-Mex Egg Scramble
Lunch: Thyme Spinach & Cheese Stuffed Mushrooms
Dinner: Unique Thai Chicken Tacos
Dessert: Rick Hot Chocolate

Day 7:
Breakfast: Italian Tomato and Feta Frittata
Lunch: Flavorful Mixed-Vegetable Lasagna
Dinner: Indian Tikka Masala Sloppy Joe Sliders
Dessert: Chewy Molasses-Pecan Wheat Berry Pudding

Week 3

Day 1:

Breakfast: Low-Carb Cauliflower Cheese "Grits"

Lunch: Yummy Crustless Quiche with Spinach & Feta

Dinner: Cheesy Turkey Meatballs

Dessert: Sweet Pineapple Upside-Down Cake

Day 2:

Breakfast: Homemade Cheesy Egg-Stuffed Bell Peppers

Lunch: Easy Slow Cooker Enchilada Casserole

Dinner: Coconut Curried Lamb

Dessert: Delicious Strawberry Pandowdy

Day 3:

Breakfast: Quinoa-Arugula Salad

Lunch: Soft Eggplant Parmesan

Dinner: Aromatic Jerk Pork Chops

Dessert: Tasty Toasted Almond Cheesecake

Day 4:

Breakfast: Broccoli Breakfast Sausage Casserole

Lunch: Healthy White Bean Cassoulet

Dinner: Homemade Chicken Bone Broth

Dessert: Crispy Chocolate Chip Cookies

Day 5:

Breakfast: Spanish Rice and Tomatoes

Lunch: Tasty Spicy Bean Burritos

Dinner: Garlic Sea Bass with Tofu

Dessert: Quick Chocolate Walnut Fudge

Day 6:

Breakfast: Harvest Rice with Mushroom & Cranberries

Lunch: Eggplant Parmesan Slices

Dinner: Lime-Cilantro Chicken Drumsticks

Dessert: Yummy Peanut Butter Cup Cake

Day 7:

Breakfast: Easy Quinoa

Lunch: Mexican Sweet Potato Enchiladas

Dinner: Tasty Tuna with Garlic Butter in Foil

Dessert: Fresh Berry Cobbler

Week 4

Day 1:

Breakfast: Pistachio Fruit Quinoa

Lunch: Classic Israeli Couscous with Chickpeas

Dinner: Balsamic Turkey Wings

Dessert: Winter Warm Gingerbread

Day 2:

Breakfast: Creamy Layered Egg Casserole

Lunch: Spicy Garlic Tofu and Vegetables

Dinner: North African Braised Beef with Almonds

Dessert: Basic Almond Golden Cake

Day 3:

Breakfast: Almond Rice Breakfast Pudding with Raisins

Lunch: Homemade Chili con "Carne"

Dinner: Braised Tender Lamb with Fennel

Dessert: Crispy Chocolate Chip Cookies

Day 4:

Breakfast: Classic French Toast Casserole

Lunch: Fresh Tomatoes with Kale and Feta

Dinner: Thick Beef Bone Broth

Dessert: Hearty Pumpkin Pie Oats

Day 5:

Breakfast: Traditional Spanakopita Frittata

Lunch: Flavorful Garlic-Parmesan Green Beans

Dinner: Parmesan Garlic Pork

Dessert: Holiday Chocolate-Covered Nut Clusters

Day 6:

Breakfast: Cheesy Potato and Egg Breakfast Casserole

Lunch: Simple Herbed Spaghetti Squash Casserole

Dinner: Herb-Garlic Turkey Legs

Dessert: Chewy Molasses-Pecan Wheat Berry Pudding

Day 7:

Breakfast: Tasty Crustless Wild Mushroom–Kale Quiche

Lunch: Simple Cheesy Ratatouille

Dinner: Homemade Salmon Ratatouille

Dessert: Rick Hot Chocolate

Chapter 1 Breakfast

Classic French Toast Casserole

Prep Time: 10 minutes | Cook Time: 4 hours | Serves: 8

6 large eggs
2 cups milk
1 teaspoon vanilla extract
1½ teaspoons ground cinnamon, divided

1 (1-pound) loaf French bread (preferably stale), cubed
4 tablespoons (½ stick) unsalted butter, at room temperature
½ cup brown sugar

1. Whisk together the eggs, milk, vanilla, and ½ teaspoon of cinnamon in the slow cooker. Submerge the bread cubes in the mixture; if necessary, put a plate on top to keep the bread submerged. Cover and refrigerate for at least 4 hours or up to overnight. 2. In a small bowl, mix the brown sugar, butter, and remaining 1 teaspoon of cinnamon. Scatter the topping over the bread mixture. 3. Cover and cook on low for 4 hours. 4. Turn off the slow cooker and let it sit for 15 minutes before serving.

Pistachio Fruit Quinoa

Prep Time: 10 minutes | Cook Time: 7-8 hours | Serves: 8

2½ cups low-fat or fat-free milk, or plant-based milk
2 cups water
2 cups quinoa, rinsed and drained
2 cups frozen raspberries

1 medium ripe banana, mashed
1 tablespoon honey
1 teaspoon ground cinnamon
1 cup shelled pistachios, chopped, for garnish

1. Combine the milk, water, quinoa, banana, honey, raspberries, and cinnamon in a 6-quart slow cooker. Cover and cook on low for 7 to 8 hours. 2. when cooking is finished, serve hot, garnished with the chopped pistachios.

Almond Rice Breakfast Pudding with Raisins

Prep Time: 10 minutes | Cook Time: 6-8 hours | Serves: 8

Nonstick cooking spray
6 cups low-fat or fat-free milk, or plant-based milk
2 cups long-grain brown rice
1 cup raisins
1 ripe banana, mashed

1 tablespoon honey, maple syrup, or sweetener of choice
2 teaspoons vanilla extract
1 teaspoon ground cinnamon
½ cup chopped almonds

1. Spray the inside of a 6-quart slow cooker with the cooking spray. Combine the milk, rice, raisins, honey, vanilla, banana, and cinnamon. Cover and cook on low for 6 to 8 hours. 2. When cooing is finished, serve hot. Top the rice with the chopped almonds and additional milk and sweetener, if desired.

Mac and Cheese with Bread Crumbs

Prep Time: 20 minutes | Cook Time: 2 to 3 hours | Serves: 8

3½ cups whole milk
1 can (12 oz) evaporated milk
1 box (16 oz) elbow macaroni
4 cups shredded Cheddar cheese (16 oz)
8 oz Kraft Velveeta cheese, cut into small cubes
½ cup shredded Parmesan cheese
2 tbsp butter

½ cup butter, melted
1 tsp Dijon mustard
¾ tsp salt
¼ tsp black pepper
⅛ tsp ground cayenne pepper
⅔ cup crispy bread crumbs

1. Spray your slow cooker cooking spray. Add in the whole milk, evaporated milk, mustard, melted butter, cayenne pepper, salt and black pepper. Whisk well. 2. Add macaroni, the cubed Velveeta cheese, 3½ cups of the Cheddar cheese and the Parmesan cheese into the slow cooker. 3. Cover and cook on low heat for 1 hour. Stir well. Cover again and cook for additional 1 to 1½ hours. The pasta must not be mushy. 4. Stir until mac and cheese is creamy. Spread the remaining ½ cup Cheddar on top. Cover and leave to rest until the cheese is melted. 5. In the meantime, in a skillet, heat 2 tablespoons butter over medium heat. Add bread crumbs; stir and cook for about 3 minutes. 6. Sprinkle over mac and cheese, and serve.

Coconut Bacon and Eggs Breakfast Casserole

Prep Time: 15 minutes | Cook Time: 5-6 hours | Serves: 8

1 tablespoon bacon fat or extra-virgin olive oil
12 eggs
1 cup coconut milk
1 pound bacon, chopped and cooked crisp
½ sweet onion, chopped

2 teaspoons minced garlic
¼ teaspoon freshly ground black pepper
⅛ teaspoon salt
Pinch red pepper flakes

1. Lightly grease the insert of the slow cooker with the bacon fat or olive oil. 2. In a medium bowl, whisk together the eggs, bacon, onion, garlic, pepper, coconut milk, salt, and red pepper flakes. Pour the mixture into the slow cooker. 3. Cover and cook on low for 5 to 6 hours. 4. Serve warm.

Cheesy Potato and Egg Breakfast Casserole

Prep Time: 10 minutes | Cook Time: 7-8 hours | Serves: 8

12 large eggs
1 cup low-fat milk
¼ teaspoon dried mustard
½ teaspoon garlic powder
½ teaspoon salt
½ teaspoon freshly ground black pepper

Nonstick cooking spray
1 (30-ounce) bag frozen hash browns, thawed in the refrigerator
1 (14-ounce) bag frozen peppers and onions, thawed in the refrigerator
6 ounces (1½ cups) 2% shredded Cheddar cheese

1. In a large bowl, whisk together the eggs, milk, garlic powder, salt, dried mustard, and pepper. 2. Spray the bowl a 6-quart slow cooker with the cooking spray. Layer one-third of the hash browns in the slow cooker followed by one-third of the peppers and onions, then one-third of the cheese. Repeat the layers two more times. 3. Slowly add the egg mixture over the top. Cover and cook on low for 7 to 8 hours. 4. Cut into 8 wedges and serve hot.

Creamy Layered Egg Casserole

Prep Time: 10 minutes | Cook Time: 4 hours | Serves: 12

1 tablespoon extra-virgin olive oil
1 pound breakfast sausage
1 zucchini, chopped
1 red bell pepper, finely chopped
½ sweet onion, chopped

12 ounces shredded cheddar cheese
12 eggs
1 cup heavy (whipping) cream
½ teaspoon salt
½ teaspoon freshly ground black pepper

1. Lightly grease the insert of the slow cooker with the olive oil. 2. Arrange half of the sausage in the bottom of the insert. Top with half of the zucchini, pepper, and onion. Top the vegetables with half of the cheese. Repeat, creating another layer. 3. In a medium bowl, whisk together the eggs, heavy cream, salt, and pepper. Pour the egg mixture over the casserole. 4. Cover and cook on low for 4 hours. 5. Serve warm.

Traditional Spanakopita Frittata

Prep Time: 10 minutes | Cook Time: 5-6 hours | Serves: 8

1 tablespoon extra-virgin olive oil
12 eggs
1 cup heavy (whipping) cream
2 teaspoons minced garlic
2 cups chopped spinach

½ cup feta cheese
Cherry tomatoes, halved, for garnish (optional)
Yogurt, for garnish (optional)
Parsley, for garnish (optional)

1. Lightly grease the insert of the slow cooker with the olive oil. 2. In a medium bowl, whisk together the eggs, garlic, spinach, heavy cream, and feta. Pour the mixture into the slow cooker. 3. Cover and cook on low heat for 5 to 6 hours. 4. Serve topped with the tomatoes, a dollop of yogurt, and parsley, if desired.

Tasty Crustless Wild Mushroom–Kale Quiche

Prep Time: 10 minutes | Cook Time: 5-6 hours | Serves: 8

1 tablespoon extra-virgin olive oil
12 eggs
1 cup heavy (whipping) cream
1 tablespoon chopped fresh thyme
1 tablespoon chopped fresh chives
¼ teaspoon freshly ground black pepper

⅛ teaspoon salt
2 cups coarsely chopped wild mushrooms (shiitake, portobello, oyster, enoki)
1 cup chopped kale
1 cup shredded swiss cheese

1. Lightly grease the insert of the slow cooker with the olive oil. 2. In a medium bowl, whisk together the eggs, heavy cream, thyme, chives, pepper, and salt. Stir in the mushrooms and kale. Pour the mixture into the slow cooker and top with the cheese. 3. Cover and cook on low 5 to 6 hours. 4. Serve warm.

Cheesy Sausage & Egg Stuffed Mushrooms

Prep Time: 15 minutes | Cook Time: 6 hours | Serves: 6

6 large eggs
1 pound mushrooms, stems minced, caps left whole
1 pound bulk breakfast sausage, or links with casings removed
1 cup chopped fresh kale
1½ cups shredded cheese of choice, divided

½ onion, minced
2 garlic cloves, minced
⅓ cup chopped walnuts
½ teaspoon kosher salt
½ teaspoon freshly ground black pepper

1. Generously coat the inside of the slow cooker insert with the butter. 2. Beat the eggs in a medium bowl, then stir in the minced mushroom stems, sausage, kale, onion, garlic, walnuts, salt, 1 cup of cheese, and pepper. 3. Spoon the mixture into the mushroom caps and place each filled cap in a single layer in the bottom of the slow cooker. 4. Sprinkle the remaining ½ cup of cheese over the top. Cover the slow cooker and cook for 6 hours on low. Serve hot.

Deep-Dish Cheese Cauliflower Crust Breakfast Pizza

Prep Time: 15 minutes | Cook Time: 6 hours | Serves: 4

2 large eggs
3 cups riced cauliflower
1 cup grated Parmesan cheese
8 ounces goat cheese, divided

½ teaspoon kosher salt
1 tablespoon extra-virgin olive oil
Grated zest of 1 lemon

1. Beat the eggs, then stir in the cauliflower, 2 ounces of goat cheese, Parmesan cheese, and the salt in a large bowl until well mixed. 2. Generously coat the inside of the slow cooker insert with the olive oil. 3. Press the cauliflower mixture in an even layer around the bottom of the cooker and extending slightly up the sides. 4. In a small bowl, stir together the remaining 6 ounces of goat cheese and the lemon zest. Dollop spoonfuls onto the cauliflower crust, distributing it evenly. 5. Put the lid on the slow cooker, but prop it slightly open with a chopstick or wooden spoon. Cook for 6 hours on low or 3 hours on high, until the edges are slightly browned. 6. When finished, turn off the cooker but let the pizza sit in it for 30 minutes before serving. Serve warm.

Creamy Overnight Pumpkin Pie

Prep Time: 10 minutes | Cook Time: 6 hours | Serves: 6

3 cups pumpkin purée
6 large eggs
¼ cup heavy (whipping) cream
2 tablespoons coconut oil
2 teaspoons pure vanilla extract
¼ cup erythritol or 2 teaspoons stevia powder

1 teaspoon ground cinnamon
1 teaspoon ground ginger
¼ teaspoon ground allspice
⅛ teaspoon ground nutmeg
Pinch kosher salt

1. Fill the slow cooker insert with 1 inch of water. Cover and turn the slow cooker on low to preheat while you prep the ingredients. 2. In a blender, combine the pumpkin, eggs, heavy cream, vanilla, erythritol, coconut oil, cinnamon, allspice, nutmeg, ginger, and salt. Process until smooth and well combined. 3. Divide the pumpkin mixture equally among 6 (½-cup) ramekins, mason jars, or yogurt jars. Carefully place the containers in the hot water in the cooker. Cover and cook for 6 hours on low. 4. When finished, serve the custards warm, or refrigerate and serve cold.

Healthy Keto Granola

Prep Time: 5 minutes | Cook Time: 2 hours | Serves: 10

⅓ cup coconut oil
1½ teaspoons pure vanilla extract or vanilla bean paste
1½ cups pumpkin seeds
1 cup unsweetened shredded coconut
½ cup almonds
½ cup walnuts

½ cup pecans
½ cup hazelnuts
½ cup sunflower seeds
½ cup erythritol or ½ teaspoon stevia powder
1 teaspoon ground cinnamon
1 teaspoon kosher salt

1. Set the slow cooker on high and let it preheat. 2. Put the coconut oil in the cooker. Once melted, stir in the vanilla. 3. Add the pumpkin seeds, almonds, walnuts, pecans, hazelnuts, coconut, and sunflower seeds. Stir to mix well, making sure all the ingredients are coated with coconut oil. 4. In a small bowl, stir together the erythritol, cinnamon, and salt. Sprinkle over the ingredients in the slow cooker. Cover and cook for 2 hours on high, stirring every 30 minutes. 5. When finished, transfer the granola to a large, rimmed baking sheet and spread it out so it cools quickly. Serve immediately or store in a covered container at room temperature for up to 3 weeks.

Classic Cheese Soufflé

Prep Time: 10 minutes | Cook Time: 2-3 hours | Serves: 8

8 ounces sharp Cheddar, shredded
8 ounces mozzarella, shredded
8 slices thin sandwich bread
Nonstick cooking spray

2 cups evaporated milk (regular, low-fat, or fat-free)
4 eggs
¼ teaspoon ground cayenne pepper

1. In a large bowl, mix the cheeses, and set aside. 2. Tear the bread into large pieces and set aside. 3. Spray a 4-quart slow cooker with nonstick cooking spray. Alternately layer the cheese and bread in the insert, beginning and ending with bread. 4. Whisk together the evaporated milk, eggs, and cayenne in a small bowl. Pour over the bread and cheese layers. Cover and cook on low for 2–3 hours. 5. When finished, serve.

Easy Spinach Quiche

Prep Time: 10 minutes | Cook Time: 2-3 hours | Serves: 6

Nonstick cooking spray
¼ teaspoon ground cayenne pepper
½ teaspoon ground nutmeg
4 eggs
½ cup shredded low-fat sharp Cheddar

6 ounces baby spinach
1½ cups evaporated milk (regular, low-fat, or fat-free)
¼ cup diced green onion
2 slices sandwich bread, cut into ½ inch cubes

1. Spray a round 4-quart slow cooker with the nonstick cooking spray. 2. In a small bowl, whisk together the cayenne, eggs, cheese, spinach, nutmeg, evaporated milk, and green onion. 3. Add the bread cubes in one layer on the bottom of the slow cooker. Add the egg mixture over the top and cover. 4. Cook for 2–3 hours on high or until the edges begin to pull away from the edge of the insert. 5. When finished, slice and lift out each slice individually.

Sweet Apple Cherry Granola Crisp

Prep Time: 10 minutes | Cook Time: 2-3 hours | Serves: 8

Cooking spray
4 crisp apples, such as Granny Smith, golden delicious, or Cortland
2 baking apples, such as gala, McIntosh, or pink lady
2 tablespoons fresh lemon juice
1 teaspoon ground cinnamon
¼ teaspoon ground cardamom

¼ cup granulated sugar
2 tablespoons cornstarch
1 cup cherry granola
¼ cup firmly packed brown sugar
¼ cup (½ stick) unsalted butter or margarine, cubed
1 cup yogurt (optional)

1. Spray the inside of a 4-quart slow cooker with cooking spray. 2. Peel, core, and chop the apples into ½" cubes. Place in a large bowl and toss with the lemon juice. 3. In a small bowl mix together the cinnamon, granulated sugar, cardamom, and cornstarch. Add to the apple mixture; stir to combine. Transfer apple/spice mixture to prepared slow cooker. 4. In a medium bowl, mix the granola with the brown sugar. Sprinkle evenly over the apple mixture. Arrange butter or margarine cubes on top. 5. Cover and cook on high for 2–3 hours. If mixture seems too liquidy, set cover ajar and cook on high for up to an additional half hour. 6. When finished, serve warm with yogurt, if desired.

Hash Brown and Sausage Casserole

Prep Time: 10 minutes | Cook Time: 3-4 hours | Serves: 8

2 tablespoons unsalted butter
1 small onion, peeled and diced
1 small green pepper, seeded and diced
1 (8-ounce) package vegetarian sausage links
8 eggs

¼ cup milk, whole, low-fat, or skim
½ teaspoon kosher salt
¼ teaspoon ground black pepper
1 (30-ounce) bag plain frozen hash brown potatoes, defrosted
1 (8-ounce) package shredded Cheddar cheese

1. Melt the butter in a small skillet over medium-high heat. Add the onion and green pepper. Cook and stir frequently, until the onions soften, about 5 minutes. 2. Push the onions to the sides and add the vegetarian sausage links. Cook for about 3 minutes or until the sausages are browned on all sides. Transfer to a 4- or 6-quart slow cooker. 3. In a large bowl, whisk together the eggs, salt, milk, and pepper. Add the hash browns and stir to completely coat the potatoes with the egg mixture, breaking up clumps, if any. 4. Pour the potato mixture over the onions and sausages. Sprinkle the cheese evenly on top. Cover and cook on high for 3–4 hours or until cheese has melted and eggs are set. 5. When finished, serve.

Authentic Shakshuka

Prep Time: 10 minutes | Cook Time: 2-3 hours | Serves: 4

1 tablespoon olive oil
1 large yellow onion, peeled and diced
2 large potatoes, peeled and cut into 1" chunks
1 red pepper, seeded and diced
4 garlic cloves, minced
1 teaspoon ground cumin
1 tablespoon sweet paprika

¼ teaspoon cayenne pepper
1 (28-ounce) can fire-roasted diced tomatoes, undrained
1 teaspoon kosher salt
4 eggs
¼ teaspoon ground black pepper
1 tablespoon parsley leaves, chopped (for garnish)

1. Heat the oil in a large skillet over medium-high heat. Add the onion and potatoes. Cook and stir frequently, for about 5 minutes, or until the onions soften. 2. Add the red pepper and garlic. Continue to sauté for another 2 minutes. 3. When finished, transfer mixture to a 4-quart slow cooker. Stir in remaining ingredients except the eggs, black pepper, and parsley. Cover and cook on low for 4 hours. 4. Carefully break the eggs on top of the tomato sauce. Do not stir in. Re-cover and continue to cook for another 10–15 minutes or until the eggs are poached to your preference. Sprinkle with the black pepper and parsley (if desired) before serving.

Fresh Pear, Apple, and Cranberry Pancake Topping

Prep Time: 5 minutes | Cook Time: 2 hours | Serves: 8

3 tart apples, thinly sliced
3 Bosc pears, thinly sliced
¾ cup fresh cranberries
1 tablespoon brown sugar

½ teaspoon ground ginger
½ teaspoon cinnamon
¼ teaspoon nutmeg
¼ teaspoon mace

1. Place all ingredients into a 3- or 4-quart slow cooker. Stir. Cook on low for 2 hours. 2. When finished, serve.

Matzonhs Spinach Pie

Prep Time: 10 minutes | Cook Time: 2-4 hours | Serves: 4-6

4 matzohs
2 cups hot water
1½ pounds fresh spinach, washed, drained well, and chopped
3 eggs, lightly beaten
1 teaspoon kosher salt

¼ teaspoon black pepper
¼ teaspoon nutmeg
¼ cup matzoh meal
1 tablespoon olive oil
1 tablespoon ground walnuts or almonds

1. Lightly spray the inside of a 4-quart slow cooker with the cooking spray. 2. Place the matzohs in a colander set in the sink. Pour the hot water over the matzohs; drain well and set aside. 3. In a large bowl, combine the spinach, eggs, salt, pepper, nutmeg, and matzoh meal. Set aside. 4. Line the prepared cooker with half of the softened matzoh, letting them come up the sides. Spread the spinach mixture on top of the matzoh layer. Cover with the remaining matzohs. Brush the matzohs with the oil and sprinkle walnuts evenly over the top. 5. Cover and cook on high for 2–4 hours. 6. When finished, serve.

Italian Tomato and Feta Frittata

Prep Time: 5 minutes | Cook Time: 6-8 hours | Serves: 8

Cooking spray
12 large eggs
1½ cups chopped fresh tomatoes
4 ounces feta cheese, crumbled
½ cup half and half

1 garlic clove, minced
1 teaspoon dried chopped onion
½ teaspoon dried basil
½ teaspoon salt
¼ teaspoon freshly ground black pepper

1. Coat a slow cooker generously with the cooking spray. 2. In a medium bowl, whisk together the eggs, feta, tomatoes, half and half, garlic, onion, basil, salt, and pepper. 3. Pour the mixture into the slow cooker. 4. Cook on low for 6 to 8 hours or on high for 3 to 4 hours, or until the eggs are set. 5. When finished, serve.

Savory Tex-Mex Egg Scramble

Prep Time: 10 minutes | Cook Time: 6-8 hours | Serves: 8

Cooking spray
12 large eggs
⅓ cup reduced-fat 2% milk
4 ounces Cheddar cheese, shredded
1 teaspoon salt
½ teaspoon freshly ground black pepper

1 small onion, chopped
2 bell peppers, seeded and chopped
1 jalapeño, seeded and chopped
¼ cup cherry tomatoes, sliced
⅓ cup chopped fresh cilantro

1. Coat a slow cooker generously with the cooking spray. 2. In a medium bowl, whisk together the eggs, milk, cheese, salt, black pepper, onion, bell peppers, jalapeño, tomatoes, and cilantro. 3. Pour the mixture into the slow cooker. 4. Cook on low for 6 to 8 hours or on high for 3 to 4 hours, or until the eggs are set. 5. Use a fork to "scramble" the mixture before serving.

Homemade Cheesy Egg-Stuffed Bell Peppers

Prep Time: 5 minutes | Cook Time: 4-6 hours | Serves: 4

4 bell peppers
4 large eggs
8 ounces Cheddar cheese, shredded

½ teaspoon salt
¼ teaspoon freshly ground black pepper

1. Cut the tops off the bell peppers and clean out the ribs and seeds. Place into a slow cooker. 2. In a small bowl, whisk together the eggs, cheese, salt, and pepper. 3. Pour ¼ of the egg mixture into each pepper. 4. Cook on low for 4 to 6 hours or on high for 2 to 3 hours, or until the eggs are fully set. 5. When finished, serve.

Homemade Cheese Egg Soufflé

Prep Time: 15 minutes | Cook Time: 5 to 6 hours | Serves: 6

Nonstick cooking spray, for coating the slow cooker
1 loaf fresh whole-wheat bread, crusts removed
1 cup shredded sharp Cheddar cheese, divided
1 cup shredded mozzarella cheese, divided
1 cup shredded Monterey Jack cheese, divided
4 tablespoons (½ stick) butter, at room temperature, divided

6 large eggs
1 cup 2% milk
1 cup half-and-half
2 teaspoons chopped fresh parsley
½ teaspoon sea salt

1. Grease your slow cooker with cooking spray. 2. Tear the bread in half, place one half in the bottom of the slow cooker, and top with ½ cup cheddar, ½ cup mozzarella, and ½ cup Monterey Jack in that order. 3. Spread small dollops of butter over the cheese, about 2 tablespoons total. 4. Repeat layering process with remaining bread, ½ cup Cheddar cheese, ½ cup mozzarella cheese, ½ cup Monterey Jack cheese, and 2 tablespoons butter. 5. Whisk together the eggs, half-and-half, milk, parsley, and salt in a large bowl. 6. Pour the egg mixture over the bread and cheese. Cover and set the heat to low. Cook for 5 to 6 hours until the eggs have set. 7. Serve the soufflé warm. 8. Refrigerate the leftovers for up to 5 days, or freeze for up to 1 month.

Low-Carb Cauliflower Cheese "Grits"

Prep Time: 10 minutes | Cook Time: 6-8 hours | Serves: 4

4 cups riced or grated cauliflower (about 1 head)
¾ cup water
¼ cup shredded Cheddar cheese

2 teaspoons butter
¼ teaspoon salt
⅛ teaspoon freshly ground black pepper

1. Add the cauliflower, water, cheese, butter, salt, and pepper to a slow cooker. Stir to mix well. 2. Cook on low for 6 to 8 hours or on high for 3 to 4 hours. 3. When finished, serve.

Spanish Rice and Tomatoes

Prep Time: 15 minutes | Cook Time: 5 to 6 hours | Serves: 4

2 cups white rice
2 cups vegetable broth
2 tablespoons extra-virgin olive oil
1 (14.5-ounce) can crushed tomatoes
1 (4-ounce) can Hatch green chiles
½ medium onion, diced

1 teaspoon sea salt
½ teaspoon ground cumin
½ teaspoon garlic powder
½ teaspoon chili powder
½ teaspoon dried oregano
Freshly ground black pepper

1. Add the rice, broth, olive oil, chiles, onion, tomatoes, salt, cumin, chili powder, garlic powder and oregano to your slow cooker. Stir until well combined and season with black pepper. 2. Cover and set the heat to low. Cook for 5 to 6 hours, fluff, and serve.

Quinoa-Arugula Salad

Prep Time: 15 minutes | Cook Time: 6 to 8 hours | Serves: 4

1½ cups quinoa, rinsed well
3 cups vegetable broth
½ teaspoon sea salt
½ teaspoon garlic powder
¼ teaspoon dried oregano
¼ teaspoon dried basil leaves

Freshly ground black pepper
3 cups arugula
½ cup diced tomatoes
⅓ cup sliced peperoncini
¼ cup freshly squeezed lemon juice
3 tablespoons extra-virgin olive oil

1. Combine the quinoa, broth, salt, oregano, garlic powder and basil in your slow cooker. Season with black pepper. 2. Cover the slow cooker and set the heat to low. Cook for 6 to 8 hours. 3. Place the tomatoes, arugula and peperoncini in a large bowl, then toss with lemon juice and olive oil. 4. When the quinoa is done, add it to the arugula salad and mix well. Serve.

Broccoli Breakfast Sausage Casserole

Prep Time: 15 minutes | Cook Time: 4 to 5 hours | Serves: 4

1 tablespoon coconut oil
6 large eggs
½ cup unsweetened almond milk
1 teaspoon Dijon mustard
1 teaspoon sea salt
1 teaspoon garlic powder

Freshly ground black pepper
1 cup broccoli florets
½ medium onion, diced
1 small sweet potato, peeled and diced
1 cup diced chicken-apple breakfast sausage

1. Grease the slow cooker with the coconut oil. 2. Whisk the eggs, almond milk, mustard, salt, and garlic powder in a medium bowl, then season with black pepper. 3. Place the broccoli, sweet potato, onion, and sausage in the slow cooker, then pour the egg mixture over the top. 4. Cover the cooker and cook at low for 4 to 5 hours, until the eggs are set and the vegetables are tender, and serve.

Easy Quinoa

Prep Time: 15 minutes | Cook Time: 4 to 6 hours | Serves: 4

2 cups quinoa, rinsed well

4 cups vegetable broth

1. Combine the quinoa and broth in your slow cooker. 2. Cover the cooker and cook at low for 4 to 6 hours. Fluff with a fork, cool, and serve.

Harvest Rice with Mushroom & Cranberries

Prep Time: 15 minutes | Cook Time: 3 hours | Serves: 4

2 cups brown rice, soaked overnight, drained, and rinsed
½ small onion, chopped
4 cups vegetable broth
2 tablespoons extra-virgin olive oil
½ teaspoon dried thyme leaves

½ teaspoon garlic powder
½ cup cooked sliced mushrooms
½ cup dried cranberries
½ cup toasted pecans

1. Add the rice, onion, olive oil, broth, thyme, and garlic powder to your slow cooker; stir until well combined. 2. Cover the cooker and cook at high for 3 hours. 3. Stir in the cranberries, mushrooms, and pecans, and serve.

Coconut Brown Rice

Prep Time: 15 minutes | Cook Time: 3 hours | Serves: 4

2 cups brown rice, soaked in water overnight, drained, and rinsed
3 cups water
1½ cups full-fat coconut milk

1 teaspoon sea salt
½ teaspoon ground ginger
Freshly ground black pepper

1. Combine the rice, water, coconut milk and ginger in your slow cooker. Season with salt and pepper. Stir until well combined. 2. Cover and cook on high for 3 hours and serve.

Chocolate Coconut Oatmeal

Prep Time: 15 minutes | Cook Time: 6 to 8 hours | Serves: 4

1 tablespoon coconut oil
2 cups rolled oats
2½ cups water
2 cups full-fat coconut milk
¼ cup unsweetened cacao powder

2 tablespoons collagen peptides
¼ teaspoon sea salt
2 tablespoons pecans
2 tablespoons unsweetened shredded coconut

1. Grease your slow cooker with the coconut oil. 2. Add the oats, water, coconut milk, collagen peptides, cacao powder, and salt to your slow cooker. Stir to combine. 3. Cover and cook on low for 6 to 8 hours. 4. Top with the pecans and coconut. Serve.

Delicious Chana Masala

Prep Time: 10 minutes | Cook Time: 6 to 7 hours | Serves: 4

1 tablespoon extra-virgin olive oil
¼ cup garlic, minced
1 tablespoon grated fresh ginger
½ teaspoon sea salt
¼ teaspoon ground black pepper
2 tablespoons garam masala
½ teaspoon ground turmeric

1 medium onion, chopped
1 (28-ounce) can crushed tomatoes, drained
2 (15-ounce) cans chickpeas, drained and rinsed
2 cups savory vegetable broth or store-bought vegetable broth
1 to 1½ cups cooked basmati, brown, or wild rice
Chopped fresh cilantro, for topping (optional)

1. Combine the olive oil, garlic, ginger, salt, black pepper, garam masala, and turmeric in your slow cooker. Cook on high for 2 to 3 minutes until fragrant, stirring occasionally. 2. Add the tomatoes, onion, and chickpeas, then pour in the broth and mix well. Cover and cook on low for 6 to 7 hours (start checking for the doneness after 6 hours), until the chickpeas are soft and easily mashed. 3. Once done cooking, sprinkle with cilantro (if using) and serve the chana masala with the rice. 4. Refrigerate leftovers for up to 5 days, or freeze for up to 2 months.

Apple Granola Toast Bake

Prep Time: 20 minutes | Cook Time: 4 to 5 hours | Serves: 8

¼ cup coconut sugar
1 teaspoon ground cinnamon
¼ teaspoon ground cardamom
10 slices whole-wheat bread, cubed
2 Granny Smith apples, peeled and diced

8 eggs
1 cup canned coconut milk
1 cup unsweetened apple juice
2 teaspoons vanilla extract
1 cup granola

1. Grease the slow cooker with vegetable oil. 2. In a small bowl, mix together the cinnamon, coconut sugar and cardamom. 3. Layer the bread, apples, and coconut sugar mixture in the slow cooker. 4. In a large bowl, whisk together the eggs, coconut milk, vanilla and apple juice. Slowly pour this mixture over the bread in the slow cooker. Top with the granola. 5. Cover and cook on low for 4 to 5 hours, or until a food thermometer registers 165°F. 6. Serve warm.

Quinoa-Veggie Egg Casserole

Prep Time: 20 minutes | Cook Time: 6 to 8 hours | Serves: 8

3 cups 2% milk
1½ cups roasted vegetable broth
11 eggs
1½ cups quinoa, rinsed and drained
3 cups chopped kale

1 leek, chopped
1 red bell pepper, seeded, and chopped
3 garlic cloves, minced
1½ cups shredded Havarti cheese

1. Grease the slow cooker with vegetable oil. 2. In a large bowl, whisk together the eggs, milk and vegetable broth. 3. Stir in the quinoa, leek, kale, bell pepper, garlic, and cheese. Pour this mixture into the slow cooker. 4. Cover and cook on low for 6 to 8 hours, or until a food thermometer registers 165°F and the mixture is set.

Honey Carrot Oatmeal

Prep Time: 20 minutes | Cook Time: 6 to 8 hours | Serves: 8

3 cups steel-cut oats
2 cups finely grated carrot
1 (8-ounce) BPA-free can unsweetened crushed pineapple in juice, undrained
2 cups almond milk
4 cups water

2 tablespoons melted coconut oil
¼ cup honey
2 teaspoons vanilla extract
¼ teaspoon salt
1 teaspoon ground cinnamon

1. Grease the slow cooker with vegetable oil. 2. Add the steel-cut oats, carrot, and pineapple to the slow cooker; stir to mix well. 3. In a medium bowl, mix together the almond milk, water, honey, vanilla, coconut oil, salt, and cinnamon. Pour this mixture into the slow cooker. 4. Cover and cook on low for 6 to 8 hours, or until the oatmeal is tender and the edges begin to brown.

Pumpkin Oatmeal

Prep Time: 15 minutes | Cook Time: 6 to 8 hours | Serves: 10

3 cups steel-cut oats
1 (16-ounce) can solid pack pumpkin
2 cups canned coconut milk
4 cups water
¼ cup honey

2 teaspoons vanilla extract
¼ teaspoon salt
1 teaspoon ground cinnamon
½ teaspoon ground ginger
1 cup granola

1. Grease the slow cooker with vegetable oil. 2. Place the oats in the slow cooker. 3. In a medium bowl, add the canned pumpkin and coconut milk with a wire whisk until well combined. 4. Then stir in the water, honey, cinnamon, salt, vanilla, and ginger. Stir to mix well. 5. Pour this mixture over the oats in the slow cooker and stir well. Spread the granola on top. 6. Cover and cook on low for 6 to 8 hours, or until the oatmeal is tender and the edges begin to brown.

Homemade Shakshuka

Prep Time: 15 minutes | Cook Time: minutes | Serves: 4

1 tablespoon extra-virgin olive oil
1 medium yellow onion, finely chopped
1 cup finely chopped peppers, such as a combination of jalapeño, poblano, and bell peppers
1 tablespoon minced garlic
1 (28-ounce) can no-salt-added crushed tomatoes, with their juices
1 teaspoon dried oregano

1 teaspoon ground cumin
1½ cups no-salt-added black beans, drained and rinsed
½ cup frozen corn, thawed
4 large eggs
Freshly ground black pepper
Sliced avocado, for garnish (optional)
Chopped fresh cilantro, for garnish (optional)

1. Combine the onion, oil, peppers, garlic, oregano, tomatoes with their juices, and cumin in your slow cooker. 2. Cover and cook on low for 8 hours, until the onion and peppers become softened. 3. Stir in beans and corn. Using the back of a spoon, make 4 indentations in the sauce, breaking an egg into each. Sprinkle some pepper over each egg. 4. Cover and cook on high for 20 to 25 minutes, until the egg whites are set but the yolks are still runny. 5. Divide the eggs and sauce between serving plates and top with avocado and cilantro (if using). 6. Refrigerate leftovers for up to 4 days. The sauce without the eggs may be frozen for up to 6 months.

Beans Salad with Red Wine Vinaigrette

Prep Time: 10 minutes | Cook Time: 3 to 4 hours | Serves: 7

3 tablespoons red wine vinegar
3 tablespoons extra-virgin olive oil
1 tablespoon minced garlic
½ teaspoon red pepper flakes (optional)
½ teaspoon adobo seasoning

1 medium red onion, finely chopped
1 (15-ounce) can no-salt-added black beans, drained and rinsed
1 (15-ounce) can no-salt-added pinto beans, drained and rinsed
1 (15-ounce) can no-salt-added cannellini beans, drained and rinsed

1. Whisk together the oil, garlic, red pepper flakes (if using), vinegar, and adobo seasoning in your slow cooker. Stir in the onion, pinto beans, black beans, and cannellini beans. 2. Cover and cook on low for 3 to 4 hours, until the flavors meld together. 3. Serve warm. 4. Refrigerate leftovers for up to 3 days or freeze for up to 6 months.

Lemon-Garlic Chickpeas

Prep Time: 5 minutes | Cook Time: 3 hours | Serves: 6

2 tablespoons extra-virgin olive oil
Grated zest and juice from 1 large lemon
1 tablespoon minced garlic

1 teaspoon dried basil
2 (15-ounce) cans no-salt-added chickpeas, drained and rinsed (about 3 cups)

1. Combine the oil, garlic, lemon zest and juice, basil, and chickpeas in your slow cooker. 2. Cover and cook on low for 3 hours. 3. Serve warm or at room temperature. 4. Refrigerate leftovers for up to 4 days or freeze for up to 6 months.

Sweet Potato Hash

Prep Time: 10 minutes | Cook Time: 6 to 8 hours | Serves: 6

Cooking spray
2 pounds sweet potatoes, peeled and shredded
1 small onion, diced
1 green or red bell pepper, diced
12 large eggs

¼ cup unsweetened almond milk
½ teaspoon salt
¼ teaspoon freshly ground black pepper
Chopped fresh herbs, for garnish (optional)

1. Grease the slow cooker with cooking spray. 2. In a medium bowl, combine the sweet potatoes, onion, and bell pepper and mix well. 3. Press the sweet potato mixture into the bottom of the slow cooker. Whisk together the eggs, almond milk, salt, and pepper in a large bowl. 4. Pour the egg mixture over the sweet potatoes in the slow cooker, making sure all the sweet potatoes are coated in the egg mixture. 5. Cover and cook on low for 6 to 8 hours. 6. Sprinkle with fresh herbs, if using, and serve.

Cheesy Potato Breakfast Casserole

Prep Time: 15 minutes | Cook Time: 6 to 8 hours | Serves: 8

¾ pound ground turkey sausage or bacon
Cooking spray
¾ (28-ounce) bag frozen Potatoes O'Brien or hash browns, thawed
1 cup chopped mushrooms
2 cups shredded Cheddar cheese

12 large eggs
¼ cup unsweetened almond milk
½ teaspoon salt
¼ teaspoon freshly ground black pepper

1. In a large skillet over medium heat, brown the ground turkey sausage. Drain off any grease. 2. Grease the slow cooker with cooking spray. 3. Arrange some of the potatoes in a single layer on the bottom of the slow cooker. 4. Spread some of the browned meat, mushrooms, and cheese on top. 5. Repeat these layers until all ingredients are used. 6. Whisk together the eggs, almond milk, salt, and black pepper in a medium bowl. 7. Pour the egg mixture over the potatoes, meat, and cheese layers, ensuring the egg mixture coats all the ingredients. 8. Cover and cook on low for 6 to 8 hours.

Apple Oatmeal

Prep Time: 5 minutes | Cook Time: 7 to 9 hours | Serves: 4

Cooking spray
1 apple, cored, peeled, and diced
1 cup steel-cut oats
2½ cups unsweetened vanilla almond milk

2 tablespoons honey or maple syrup
½ teaspoon vanilla extract
1 teaspoon ground cinnamon

1. Grease the slow cooker with cooking spray. 2. Add all the ingredients to the slow cooker and mix well. 3. Cover and cook on low for 7 to 9 hours. Serve warm.

Easy Oatmeal

Prep Time: 5 minutes | Cook Time: 3 hours | Serves: 6

⅓ cup canola oil
1 large egg
¾ cup milk
2 cups quick-cooking oats

½ cup sugar
1½ teaspoons baking powder
½ teaspoon salt

1. Pour the canola oil into the slow cooker, tilting it so that it fully covers the bottom and sides of the pot. 2. Whisk the egg in a medium bowl. Add the milk, oats, baking powder, sugar, and salt and mix well. Pour the mixture into the slow cooker. 3. Cover and cook on low for 3 hours. Serve.

Chapter 2 Vegetables and Sides

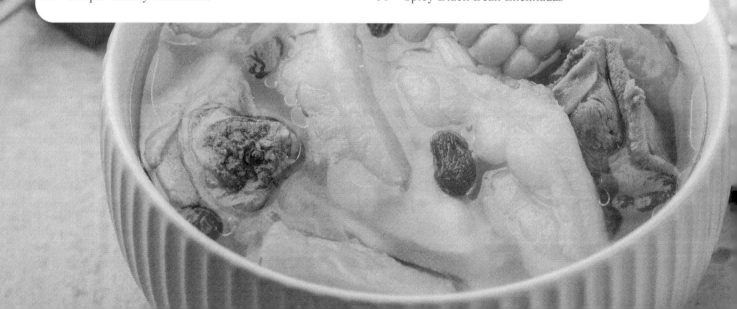

Healthy Vegan Jambalaya

Prep Time: 15 minutes | Cook Time: 6-8 hours | Serves: 6

5 cups low-sodium vegetable broth
1 (15-ounce) can red kidney beans, drained and rinsed
2 cups diced fresh tomatoes with their juices, or 1 (14.5-ounce) can
no-salt-added diced tomatoes
2 cups long-grain brown rice
1 cup ½-inch round okra slices
1 cup chopped cashews
2 celery stalks, diced
1 green bell pepper, diced

1 medium onion, diced
4 garlic cloves, minced
2 tablespoons cayenne hot sauce (or to taste)
1 tablespoon extra-virgin olive oil
1 tablespoon smoked paprika
1 tablespoon ground cumin
1 teaspoon dried thyme
1 teaspoon dried oregano

1. Combine all the ingredients in a 6-quart slow cooker. Cover and cook on low for 6 to 8 hours, until the vegetables and rice are tender and the sauce has thickened. If the rice is too dry during cooking, add more broth or water. 2. When finished, serve hot.

Classic Barley and Chickpea Risotto

Prep Time: 10 minutes | Cook Time: 6-7 hours | Serves: 8

5 cups low-sodium vegetable broth
2 cups hulled barley, rinsed
1 (15-ounce) can chickpeas, drained and rinsed
1 cup water
3 carrots, minced
1 onion, finely chopped

½ head cauliflower, cut into small pieces
4 garlic cloves, minced
1 teaspoon dried thyme
1½ tablespoons freshly squeezed lemon juice
⅓ cup grated Parmesan cheese
4 tablespoons chopped fresh parsley, for garnish (optional)

1. Put the broth, barley, water, carrots, onion, cauliflower, chickpeas, garlic, and thyme in a 6-quart slow cooker. Stir to combine. Cover and cook on low for 6 to 7 hours, or until the barley is tender and has absorbed most of the liquid. 2. Stir in the lemon juice and Parmesan cheese. 3. When finished, serve garnished with the fresh parsley (if using).

Fiber-Rich Potato and Corn Chowder

Prep Time: 10 minutes | Cook Time: 7-8 hours | Serves: 8

1½ pounds red potatoes, diced
1 (16-ounce) package frozen corn
2 medium carrots, chopped
1 large onion, chopped
3 tablespoons all-purpose flour
5 cups low-sodium vegetable broth

2 teaspoons dried thyme
4 garlic cloves, minced
1 tablespoon extra-virgin olive oil
Salt
Freshly ground black pepper
1 (12-ounce) can evaporated nonfat milk

1. Place the potatoes, corn, carrots, and onion into a 6-quart slow cooker. Stir in the flour and gently toss to combine. Stir in the broth, thyme, garlic, and olive oil. Season with the salt and pepper. 2. Cover and cook on low for 7 to 8 hours. Thirty minutes before serving, stir in the evaporated milk and continue cooking until heated through. 3. Serve immediately.

Simple Spaghetti Squash

Prep Time: 5 minutes | Cook Time: 7-8 hours | Serves: 4

1 spaghetti squash (choose a size that will fit in your slow cooker)

2 cups water

1. Wash your squash with the soap and water, and rinse well. With a skewer or fork, puncture 5 or 6 holes in the squash and place it in the slow cooker. Pour in the water. Cover and cook on low for 7 to 8 hours. 2. When finished, carefully remove the squash to a cutting board and allow it to cool for 15 to 20 minutes. Cut the squash in half, and remove and discard the seeds. Using two forks, scrape out the squash strands and put them in a bowl.

Fresh Corn On the Cob

Prep Time: 10 minutes | Cook Time: 4-5 hours | Serves: 8

8 corn ears, husked
1 tablespoon extra-virgin olive oil
1 teaspoon freshly ground black pepper
1 teaspoon chili powder
¾ cup water

1 small onion, chopped
2 garlic cloves, minced
Butter (optional)
Fresh cilantro (optional)

1. Lightly brush the corn with the olive oil. Season the ears with the black pepper and chili powder and put them in a 6-quart slow cooker. 2. Add the water along with the onion and garlic. Cover and cook on low for 4 to 5 hours, until the corn is bright yellow. 3. When finished, drain and serve, with the butter and fresh cilantro, if desired.

Basil Roasted Peppers

Prep Time: 10 minutes | Cook Time: 5-6 hours | Serves: 8

Nonstick cooking spray
2 medium yellow bell peppers, halved
2 medium green bell peppers, halved
4 medium red bell peppers, halved

1 large onion, thinly sliced
1 tablespoon extra-virgin olive oil
2 teaspoons dried basil
¼ teaspoon salt

1. Spray the inside of a 6-quart slow cooker with the cooking spray. Add the peppers, onion, olive oil, basil, and salt. Cover and cook on low for 5 to 6 hours. 2. Turn off the slow cooker and remove the lid. Allow the peppers to cool. Grasp a pepper skin at an edge and gently tug to remove it in one piece. If it doesn't come off easily, use a paring knife. Repeat with remaining peppers. 3. Serve immediately with your favorite entrée or store the peppers in an airtight container in the refrigerator for up to 4 days.

Delicious Ratatouille

Prep Time: 10 minutes | Cook Time: 7-8 hours | Serves: 8

2 large onions, halved and sliced
1 large eggplant, peeled and cut into 2-inch cubes
2 medium zucchini, sliced
2 yellow summer squash, sliced
2 bell peppers (any color), cut into strips
4 garlic cloves, minced

2 large tomatoes, cut into wedges
2 portobello mushrooms, gills and stem removed, sliced
2 teaspoons herbes de Provence, divided
2 tablespoons extra-virgin olive oil, divided
1 (6-ounce) can tomato paste, divided
⅛ teaspoon sugar (optional)

1. Layer half of the onions, eggplant, zucchini, squash, peppers, garlic, tomatoes, and mushrooms, in this order, in the bottom of a 6-quart slow cooker. Sprinkle with 1 teaspoon herbes de Provence and 1 tablespoon olive oil. Dot with half the tomato paste and a sprinkle of the sugar (if using). Repeat the layering process. Cover and cook on low for 7 to 8 hours. 2. When cooking is finished, serve hot, with a sprinkle of Parmesan cheese, if desired, on a baguette, over pasta or pizza, or with your favorite entrée.

Homemade Rosemary-Maple Beets

Prep Time: 5 minutes | Cook Time: 6-8 hours | Serves: 6

Nonstick cooking spray
24 baby beets, whole, scrubbed and peeled (or 12 large, quartered)
¼ cup pure maple syrup
¼ cup balsamic vinegar
2 tablespoons extra-virgin olive oil

4 garlic cloves, minced
2 shallots, minced
1 tablespoon minced fresh rosemary, plus additional for garnish
1 teaspoon dried rosemary

1. Spray the inside of a 4- or 6-quart slow cooker with the cooking spray. Place the beets in the slow cooker. 2. In a small bowl, whisk together the maple syrup, fresh rosemary, vinegar, olive oil, garlic, shallots, and dried rosemary. 3. Cover and cook on low for 7 to 8 hours, until the beets are tender. Remove the beets and slice. Serve, garnished with additional rosemary leaves, if desired.

Nutritious Sweet-Braised Red Cabbage

Prep Time: 15 minutes | Cook Time: 7-8 hours | Serves: 8

1 tablespoon extra-virgin olive oil
1 small red cabbage, coarsely shredded (about 6 cups)
½ sweet onion, thinly sliced
¼ cup apple cider vinegar
3 tablespoons granulated erythritol
2 teaspoons minced garlic
½ teaspoon ground nutmeg

⅛ teaspoon ground cloves
2 tablespoons butter
Salt, for seasoning
Freshly ground black pepper, for seasoning
½ cup chopped walnuts, for garnish
½ cup crumbled blue cheese, for garnish
Pink peppercorns, for garnish (optional)

1. Lightly grease the insert of the slow cooker with the olive oil. 2. Add the cabbage, onion, apple cider vinegar, erythritol, garlic, nutmeg, and cloves to the insert, stirring to mix well. 3. Break off little slices of butter and scatter them on top of the cabbage mixture. 4. Cover and cook on low for 7 to 8 hours. 5. Season with the salt and pepper. 6. Serve topped with the walnuts, blue cheese, and peppercorns (if desired).

Traditional Ratatouille

Prep Time: 15 minutes | Cook Time: 6 hours | Serves: 6

3 tablespoons extra-virgin olive oil, divided
2 zucchinis, diced
1 red bell pepper, diced
1 yellow bell pepper, diced
1 cup diced pumpkin
½ sweet onion, diced

3 teaspoons minced garlic
¼ teaspoon salt
¼ teaspoon freshly ground black pepper
Pinch red pepper flakes
1 (14-ounce) can diced tomatoes
1 cup crumbled goat cheese, for garnish

1. Lightly grease the insert of the slow cooker with 1 tablespoon of the olive oil. 2. Add the red and yellow bell peppers, zucchini, pumpkin, onion, garlic, salt, pepper, and red pepper flakes to the insert, and toss to combine. 3. Add the remaining 2 tablespoons of the olive oil and the tomatoes and stir. 4. Cover and cook on low for 6 hours. 5. Serve topped with the goat cheese.

Tasty North African Vegetable Stew

Prep Time: 15 minutes | Cook Time: 7-8 hours | Serves: 6

1 tablespoon extra-virgin olive oil
2 cups diced pumpkin
2 cups chopped cauliflower
1 red bell pepper, diced
½ sweet onion, diced
2 teaspoons minced garlic

2 cups coconut milk
2 tablespoons natural peanut butter
1 tablespoon ground cumin
1 teaspoon ground coriander
¼ cup chopped cilantro, for garnish

1. Lightly grease the insert of the slow cooker with the olive oil. 2. Add the pumpkin, cauliflower, bell pepper, onion, and garlic to the insert. 3. In a small bowl, whisk together the coconut milk, peanut butter, cumin, and coriander until smooth. 4. Pour the coconut milk mixture over the vegetables in the insert. 5. Cover and cook on low for 7 to 8 hours. 6. Serve topped with the cilantro.

Flavorful Mixed-Vegetable Lasagna

Prep Time: 20 minutes | Cook Time: 7-8 hours | Serves: 6

3 tablespoons extra-virgin olive oil, divided
1 cup sliced mushrooms
2 cups simple marinara sauce
2 zucchinis, thinly sliced lengthwise
2 cups shredded kale

1 tablespoon chopped basil
8 ounces ricotta cheese
8 ounces goat cheese
2 cups shredded mozzarella cheese

1. Lightly grease the insert of the slow cooker with 1 tablespoon olive oil. 2. In a large skillet over medium-high heat, heat the remaining 2 tablespoons of the olive oil. add the mushrooms and sauté until they are softened, about 5 minutes. 3. Stir the marinara sauce into the mushrooms and stir to combine. 4. Pour about one-third of the sauce into the insert. Arrange one-third of the zucchini strips over the sauce. Top with one-third of the kale. sprinkle half of both the ricotta and goat cheese over the kale. Repeat with the sauce, zucchini, kale, ricotta, and goat cheese to create another layer. 5. Top with the remaining zucchini strips and the sauce. Sprinkle the mozzarella cheese on top. 6. Cover and cook on low for 7 to 8 hours. 7. Serve warm.

Thyme Spinach & Cheese Stuffed Mushrooms

Prep Time: 15 minutes | Cook Time: 6 hours | Serves: 6

2 tablespoons unsalted butter, ghee, or extra-virgin olive oil
3 large eggs
2 cups shredded Gruyère cheese, divided
½ cup chopped walnuts, plus more for garnish
1½ pounds cremini or button mushrooms, stems minced, caps left whole

2 cups chopped spinach
½ onion, minced
2 garlic cloves, minced
1 tablespoon fresh thyme leaves, plus more for garnish
½ teaspoon kosher salt
½ teaspoon freshly ground black pepper

1. Generously coat the inside of the slow cooker insert with the butter. 2. In a medium bowl, beat the eggs, then stir in 1½ cups of Gruyère cheese, ½ cup of walnuts, the mushroom stems, spinach, onion, garlic, 1 tablespoon of thyme, salt, and pepper. 3. Spoon the mixture into the mushroom caps and place each filled cap in a single layer in the bottom of the slow cooker. 4. Sprinkle the remaining ½ cup of Gruyère cheese over the top. Cover and cook for 6 hours on low. 5. When finished, serve hot, garnished with the additional thyme and chopped walnuts.

Cheesy Balsamic Brussels Sprouts with Pine Nuts

Prep Time: 10 minutes | Cook Time: 6 hours | Serves: 6

1 pound Brussels sprouts, halved
2 tablespoons coconut oil
Kosher salt
Freshly ground black pepper
2 tablespoons unsalted butter, cubed

2 tablespoons balsamic vinegar
2 tablespoons erythritol
2 cups grated Parmesan cheese
¼ cup toasted pine nuts

1. In the slow cooker, combine the Brussels sprouts and coconut oil. Season with the pepper and salt and stir to mix. 2. Top with the butter. Cover and cook for 6 hours on low or 3 hours on high. 3. Combine the balsamic vinegar and erythritol over medium heat and bring to a boil in a small saucepan. Reduce the heat a bit and simmer for about 8 minutes until the liquid is thick and syrupy. 4. To serve, drizzle the balsamic glaze over the Brussels sprouts and serve hot, garnished with the Parmesan cheese and pine nuts.

Yummy Crustless Quiche with Spinach & Feta

Prep Time: 10 minutes | Cook Time: 7 hours | Serves: 6

1 tablespoon unsalted butter or ghee, at room temperature
10 large eggs
1 cup heavy (whipping) cream
2 cups spinach, chopped
¾ cup crumbled feta cheese

½ cup grated Parmesan cheese
2 garlic cloves, minced
½ teaspoon freshly ground black pepper
¼ teaspoon kosher salt
¼ cup grated sharp Cheddar cheese

1. Coat the inside of the slow cooker insert with the butter. 2. In the insert, whisk together the eggs and heavy cream. 3. Stir in the spinach, feta and Parmesan cheeses, garlic, pepper, and salt. 4. Sprinkle the Cheddar cheese over the top. Cover and cook for 7 hours on low. 5. When cooking is finished, serve hot, warm, or at room temperature.

Soft Eggplant Parmesan

Prep Time: 10 minutes | Cook Time: 8 hours | Serves: 6

2 tablespoons coconut oil
2 cups tomato sauce
8 ounces mascarpone cheese
8 ounces eggplant, peeled and thinly sliced

3 cups shredded fontina cheese
1 cup grated Parmesan cheese
1 cup coarsely ground almond meal

1. Coat the inside of the slow cooker insert with the coconut oil. 2. In a medium bowl, stir together the tomato sauce and mascarpone. Coat the bottom of the insert with ½ cup of sauce. 3. Arrange several eggplant slices in a single layer, or slightly overlapping, over the sauce. 4. Top with a bit of fontina cheese, a sprinkling of almond meal, a bit of Parmesan cheese, and more sauce. Continue layering until you've used all the ingredients, ending with a layer of sauce, then cheese, and then almond meal. Cover and cook for 8 hours on low or 4 hours on high. Serve hot.

Easy Slow Cooker Enchilada Casserole

Prep Time: 15 minutes | Cook Time: 6 hours | Serves: 6

1 tablespoon coconut oil
4 large eggs
2 cups sour cream
12 ounces cream cheese, at room temperature
1½ cups grated sharp Cheddar cheese, divided
1 cup heavy (whipping) cream
1 teaspoon dried oregano

1 teaspoon kosher salt
2 (7-ounce) cans whole roasted green chiles, drained and seeded
1 pound frozen spinach, thawed
1 cup enchilada sauce
¼ cup chopped fresh cilantro
4 scallions, sliced

1. Coat the inside of the slow cooker insert with the coconut oil. 2. In a large bowl, beat the eggs, then whisk in the sour cream, cream cheese, 1 cup of Cheddar cheese, heavy cream, oregano, and salt. 3. Lay several strips of green chiles in a single layer on the bottom of the slow cooker to cover it. 4. Dollop one-third of the cheese mixture on top, distributing it evenly. Spread it out with the back of the spoon. 5. Top with one-third of the spinach, and then 1 cup of enchilada sauce. Repeat twice more with the remaining ingredients. 6. Sprinkle the remaining ½ cup of Cheddar cheese over the top layer. Cover and cook for 6 hours on low or 3 hours on high. Serve hot, garnished with the cilantro and scallions.

Eggplant Parmesan Slices

Prep Time: 15 minutes | Cook Time: 4-5 hours | Serves: 4

2 medium-sized eggplants, peeled and cut into ½-inch slices
½ cup plus ½ teaspoon kosher salt, divided
3¼ cups Marinara Sauce, divided
½ cup plain toasted bread crumbs
½ teaspoon dried oregano
1 teaspoon dried basil

¼ teaspoon ground black pepper
1 large egg, lightly beaten
½ cup grated Parmesan cheese
1 (12-ounce) package mozzarella cheese, shredded
4 large basil leaves, chopped (for garnish)

1. Place the eggplant slices in a colander in the sink. Use the ½ cup of kosher salt to evenly salt both sides of each eggplant slice. Let sit for 30 minutes, then rinse the slices and pat dry with paper towels. 2. Meanwhile, coat a 4-quart slow cooker with ¼ cup of the marinara sauce. Set aside. 3. In a medium bowl, combine the oregano, basil, bread crumbs, remaining ½ teaspoon kosher salt, and the black pepper. 4. Place the beaten egg in a medium bowl. Dip each eggplant slice into the beaten egg, then into the bread crumb mixture. 5. Layer a third of the eggplant slices in the prepared slow cooker. Top with a third each of the Parmesan cheese, the mozzarella cheese, and a cup of the marinara sauce. Repeat layering two more times. 6. Cover and cook on low for 4–5 hours or until the eggplant is tender. Sprinkle with the fresh basil before serving, if desired.

Fresh Tomatoes with Kale and Feta

Prep Time: 10 minutes | Cook Time: 4-6 hours | Serves: 6

Cooking spray
1 cup chopped kale
3 pounds tomatoes, sliced
¼ cup balsamic vinegar

1 tablespoon extra-virgin olive oil
½ teaspoon salt
¼ teaspoon freshly ground black pepper
1 cup crumbled feta cheese

1. Coat a slow cooker generously with the cooking spray. 2. Place the kale in the bottom of the slow cooker. Top with the tomato slices. 3. Mix together the salt, olive oil, balsamic vinegar, and pepper in a small bowl. Pour the mixture over the top of the kale and tomatoes. 4. Cook on low for 4 to 6 hours or on high for 2 to 3 hours. 5. When finished, top with the crumbled feta and serve.

Flavorful Garlic-Parmesan Green Beans

Prep Time: 10 minutes | Cook Time: 4-6 hours | Serves: 6

3 pounds green beans, trimmed
⅓ cup low-sodium chicken broth
4 garlic cloves, minced
⅔ cup shaved Parmesan cheese

½ teaspoon salt
¼ teaspoon freshly ground black pepper
1 tablespoon unsalted butter, cut into small pieces

1. Place the green beans into a slow cooker. 2. Pour the broth over the top. 3. Sprinkle the garlic, salt, Parmesan, and pepper over the top. 4. Top with the pieces of butter. 5. Cook on low for 4 to 6 hours or on high for 2 to 3 hours. 6. When finished, serve.

Tasty Spicy Bean Burritos

Prep Time: 10 minutes | Cook Time: 3-4 hours | Serves: 8

½ red pepper, seeded and diced
½ green pepper, seeded and diced
2 cups Vegetarian Refried Beans
1 (15-ounce) can black beans, rinsed and drained
1 cup frozen corn, defrosted
1 cup salsa or taco sauce

2 chipotle chilies in adobo sauce (from 7-ounce can), chopped
2 teaspoons adobo sauce (from same can)
1 (8-ounce) package shredded Cheddar or taco blend cheese, divided
8 burrito-size flour tortillas
½ cup sour cream (for garnish)
4 scallions, green parts thinly sliced (for garnish)

1. In a 4-quart slow cooker, stir together the diced red and green peppers, refried beans, black beans, corn, adobo sauce, salsa, chilies, and 1 cup of the cheese. Cover and cook on low for 3–4 hours, stirring after 2 hours. 2. Spread a layer of the bean mixture down the center of each tortilla, leaving about an inch margin on each end. 3. Sprinkle the remaining cheese over the bean mixture. Spread a dollop of sour cream and sprinkle with scallions, if desired. Fold margin ends over, then roll up each burrito and serve immediately.

Simple Herbed Spaghetti Squash Casserole

Prep Time: 15 minutes | Cook Time: 4-6 hours | Serves: 6

1 (2-pound) spaghetti squash
Cooking spray
1 cup low-sodium or no-salt-added diced tomatoes
¼ teaspoon oregano
¼ teaspoon rosemary
¼ teaspoon thyme
¼ teaspoon parsley

¼ teaspoon basil
½ teaspoon salt
¼ teaspoon freshly ground black pepper
4 ounces mozzarella cheese, shredded
⅓ cup grated Parmesan cheese
¼ cup water

1. Pierce the spaghetti squash all over with a knife, place in a microwave-safe dish, and microwave for 7 to 10 minutes or until soft. Be careful removing the squash from the microwave because it will be very hot. 2. Cut the squash in half and scoop out and discard the seeds. 3. Use a fork to scrape out the spaghetti-like strands into a large bowl. 4. Coat a slow cooker generously with the cooking spray. 5. Add the spaghetti squash strands, tomatoes, oregano, thyme, parsley, basil, salt, rosemary, pepper, mozzarella, Parmesan, and water to the slow cooker. Stir to mix well. 6. Cook on low for 4 to 6 hours or on high for 2 to 3 hours.

Homemade Chili con "Carne"

Prep Time: 10 minutes | Cook Time: 5 hours | Serves: 4

½ cup onion, diced
½ cup bell pepper, diced
1 (12-ounce) package frozen veggie burger crumbles
2 cloves garlic, minced
1 (15-ounce) can kidney beans, rinsed and drained
2 cups Vegetable Broth
1 tablespoon chili powder
½ tablespoon chipotle powder

½ tablespoon cumin
1 teaspoon thyme
1 tablespoon oregano
2 cups fresh tomatoes, diced
1 tablespoon tomato paste
1 tablespoon cider vinegar
2 teaspoons salt
Vegan Beef

1. In a 4-quart slow cooker, add all ingredients. Cover and cook on low heat for 5 hours. 2. When finished, serve.

Classic Israeli Couscous with Chickpeas

Prep Time: 10 minutes | Cook Time: 4 hours | Serves: 8

1 tablespoon olive oil
1 cup Israeli couscous
2 (15-ounce) cans chickpeas, drained and rinsed
1 cup water
2 teaspoons kosher salt

1 teaspoon black pepper
½ teaspoon ground cumin
½ teaspoon ground coriander
5 cloves garlic, minced
¼ cup parsley leaves, chopped (for garnish)

1. Heat the oil in a small skillet over medium heat. Sauté the couscous until it starts to brown, about 4–5 minutes. 2. Transfer the couscous to a 4-quart slow cooker. Add all remaining ingredients except parsley. Cover and cook on low heat for 4 hours. 3. Sprinkle with the parsley leaves, if desired, before serving.

Mexican Sweet Potato Enchiladas

Prep Time: 10 minutes | Cook Time: 1-2 hours | Serves: 8

2½ tablespoons olive oil, divided
1 onion, chopped
3 garlic cloves, minced
2 jalapeño peppers, seeded and minced
2 cups Vegetarian Refried Beans
1 tablespoon chili powder
1 teaspoon ground cumin

½ teaspoon salt
⅛ teaspoon pepper
1 (20-ounce) can sweet potatoes, drained and chopped
1½ cups salsa, divided
12 (10-inch) flour tortillas
2½ cups shredded Cheddar cheese, divided
2 cups Enchilada Sauce

1. Grease the inside of a 4- to 6-quart slow cooker with ½ tablespoon of the olive oil. 2. In a large skillet, heat the remaining olive oil over medium heat. When hot, add the onion. Cook and stir occasionally, until the onions are softened, about 5 minutes. Add the garlic and jalapeños and stir for another minute. 3. Add the refried beans, chili powder, salt, cumin, and pepper and bring the mixture to a simmer. Add the sweet potatoes and ½ cup salsa; remove from the heat. 4. Place the tortillas on a clean work surface. Divide the sweet potato mixture among them; top each with 2 tablespoons of Cheddar cheese. Roll up, enclosing the filling. 5. In a medium bowl, combine the remaining 1 cup salsa with the enchilada sauce and mix well. Place ½ cup sauce in the prepared cooker. Top with the enchiladas, then pour the remaining sauce evenly over the enchiladas. 6. Cover and cook on high for 1–2 hours. Uncover and top with the remaining 1 cup cheese. Cover and continue cooking for another hour. Serve immediately.

Healthy White Bean Cassoulet

Prep Time: 10 minutes | Cook Time: 8-10 hours | Serves: 8

1 pound dried cannellini beans
2 cups boiling water
1 ounce dried porcini mushrooms
2 leeks, sliced
1 teaspoon canola oil
2 parsnips, diced
2 carrots, diced
2 stalks celery, diced

½ teaspoon ground fennel
1 teaspoon crushed rosemary
1 teaspoon dried chervil
⅛ teaspoon cloves
¼ teaspoon salt
¼ teaspoon freshly ground black pepper
2 cups Vegetable Broth

1. Using Dried Beans: Dried the beans must be soaked overnight and boiled for at least 10 minutes before being added to a slow cooker, if you prefer to use them over canned beans. 2. The night before making the soup, place the beans in a 4-quart slow cooker. Fill with water to 1" below the top of the insert. Soak overnight. 3. Drain the beans and return them to the slow cooker. 4. In a heat-proof bowl, pour the 2 cups of boiling water over the dried mushrooms and let them soak for 15 minutes. 5. Slice only the white and light green parts of the leeks into ¼" rounds. Cut the rounds in half. 6. In a nonstick skillet, heat the oil; add the parsnip, carrots, celery, and leeks. Sauté for 1 minute, just until the color of the vegetables brightens. 7. Add the vegetables to the slow cooker along with the spices. Add the mushrooms, their soaking liquid, and the broth; stir. 8. Cook on low for 8–10 hours.

Spicy Garlic Tofu and Vegetables

Prep Time: 15 minutes | Cook Time: 2-3 hours | Serves: 4-6

Cooking spray
2 medium onions
1 medium carrot
3 garlic cloves, minced
¼ cup hoisin sauce
2 tablespoons rice wine vinegar
1 tablespoon soy sauce
2 teaspoons Sriracha sauce

2 teaspoons ground ginger
¼ teaspoon five-spice powder
2 tablespoons brown sugar
1 (1-pound) package extra-firm tofu, drained well and sliced into ½" cubes
3 cups cooked brown or white rice
1 tablespoon toasted sesame seeds (for garnish)

1. Lightly spray the inside of a 4-quart slow cooker with the cooking spray. 2. Peel the onions. Cut each in half, then thinly slice. Peel the carrot, then thinly slice on the diagonal. Place in the prepared slow cooker. 2. In a small mixing bowl, stir together the remaining ingredients except the tofu, rice, and sesame seeds. Pour into the slow cooker and mix with the vegetables. 3. Add the tofu and gently stir until the tofu is completely coated with the sauce. Cover and cook on low for 5 hours or on high for 2½–3 hours. 4. Ladle the tofu and vegetables over cooked rice. Sprinkle evenly with the sesame seeds, if desired.

Simple Cheesy Ratatouille

Prep Time: 5 minutes | Cook Time: 4-6 hours | Serves: 8

1 pound eggplant, peeled and chopped
1 cup grated Parmesan cheese
1 large onion, chopped
1 medium zucchini, chopped
1 bell pepper, seeded and chopped
1 (28-ounce) can low-sodium or no-salt-added diced tomatoes
2 garlic cloves, minced

1 tablespoon extra-virgin olive oil
½ teaspoon salt
½ teaspoon tarragon
½ teaspoon rosemary
½ teaspoon thyme
½ teaspoon basil

1. Add the eggplant, cheese, onion, bell pepper, tomatoes, zucchini, garlic, olive oil, salt, tarragon, rosemary, thyme, and basil to the slow cooker. Stir to mix well. 2. Cook on low for 4 to 6 hours or on high for 2 to 3 hours. 3. When finished, serve.

Rosemary Balsamic Beets

Prep Time: 15 minutes | Cook Time: 6 to 8 hours | Serves: 6

4 to 6 medium beets (they need to fit snugly in the bottom of your slow cooker), chopped
½ cup balsamic vinegar
1 cup apple juice

½ teaspoon garlic powder
½ teaspoon dried rosemary
Freshly ground black pepper

1. Combine the beets, vinegar, garlic powder, apple juice, and rosemary in your slow cooker, and season with black pepper. 2. Cover and cook on low for 6 to 8 hours and serve.

Spiced Cauliflower

Prep Time: 15 minutes | Cook Time: 3 to 4 hours | Serves: 4

1 large head cauliflower, leaves and large stem removed
½ medium onion, diced
2 tablespoons extra-virgin olive oil
½ teaspoon sea salt
½ teaspoon garlic powder

½ teaspoon ground ginger
½ teaspoon curry powder
¼ teaspoon ground turmeric
¼ teaspoon ground cumin
⅛ teaspoon cayenne pepper

1. Chop the cauliflower into small florets and add to the slow cooker with the onion. 2. Combine the olive oil, ginger, curry powder, salt, garlic powder, turmeric, cumin, and cayenne in a small bowl. Whisk into a paste. Brush the spice paste over the cauliflower. 3. Cover and cook on low for 3 to 4 hours and serve.

Aromatic Lentil Bolognese

Prep Time: 15 minutes | Cook Time: 5½ to 6½ hours | Serves: 4

1 tablespoon extra-virgin olive oil
2 carrots, grated
1 celery stalk, minced
1 small onion, diced
½ teaspoon garlic powder
4 cups diced tomatoes
2 cups vegetable broth
1 cup lentils, soaked in water overnight, drained, and rinsed well

1 bay leaf
½ teaspoon dried oregano
½ teaspoon dried basil leaves
½ teaspoon sea salt
¼ teaspoon red pepper flakes
¼ teaspoon ground nutmeg
Freshly ground black pepper

1. Grease the slow cooker with olive oil. Add in the carrots, onion, celery, and garlic powder. 2. Cover and cook on high for 30 minutes. 3. Stir in the tomatoes, broth, bay leaf, lentils, oregano, nutmeg basil, salt and red pepper flakes, then season with black pepper. Re-cover and cook on low for 5 to 6 hours. 4. Remove and discard the bay leaf before serving.

Maple-Mustard Brussels Sprouts

Prep Time: 15 minutes | Cook Time: 3 to 4 hours | Serves: 4

1 pound Brussels sprouts, ends trimmed
2 tablespoons maple syrup
1 tablespoon Dijon mustard

½ teaspoon garlic powder
½ teaspoon sea salt
¼ cup water

1. Combine the Brussels sprouts, mustard, maple syrup, salt, garlic powder and water in your slow cooker. Toss well. 2. Cover and cook on low for 3 to 4 hours and serve.

Lentil Potpie

Prep Time: 15 minutes | Cook Time: 6 to 7 hours | Serves: 6

1 tablespoon extra-virgin olive oil
3 cups savory vegetable broth or store-bought vegetable broth, divided
2 tablespoons cornstarch
1 pound white potatoes, peeled and diced
1 medium white or yellow onion, diced
1½ cups sliced carrots
1 cup sliced celery
8 ounces cremini mushrooms, stemmed and sliced
2 teaspoons minced garlic
1 teaspoon sea salt

½ teaspoon ground black pepper
1 teaspoon dried thyme
1 or 2 bay leaves
1 cup dried green lentils
1 cup frozen corn kernels
¼ cup sliced scallions, both white and green parts
¾ cup 2 percent milk
1 tablespoon white-wine vinegar or lemon juice
1 (16.3-ounce) container flaky biscuit dough (such as Pillsbury Grands! Southern Home-style), cut into small wedges

1. Grease the slow cooker with the olive oil. 2. In a medium bowl, whisk together 1½ cups of broth and the cornstarch. 3. Combine the potatoes, onion, celery, mushrooms, carrots, garlic, salt, black pepper, bay leaf, thyme, and lentils in the slow cooker. 4. Pour the broth and cornstarch mixture and the remaining 1½ cups of broth into the slow cooker. Stir to mix well. Cover and cook on low for 6 hours, until the vegetables and lentils are tender. 5. Then stir in the corn, milk, vinegar, scallions, and biscuit dough. Cover and cook for 45 minutes longer, until the biscuit wedges have cooked through. 6. Once done cooking, discard the bay leaf and serve the potpie warm. 7. Refrigerate leftovers for up to 1 week, or freeze for up to 1 month.

Mushroom Pilaf

Prep Time: 10 minutes | Cook Time: 6 to 8 hours | Serves: 6

3 tablespoons extra-virgin olive oil, divided
2 cups wild rice, rinsed and drained
1 medium white onion, diced
1¼ cups sliced cremini mushrooms

4 cups homemade or store-bought chicken broth
½ teaspoon sea salt
½ teaspoon ground black pepper
1 teaspoon dried thyme

1. Grease the bottom and sides of the slow cooker with 1 tablespoon of olive oil. 2. Add the rice, mushrooms, onion, broth, salt, thyme and black pepper. Cover and cook on low for 6 to 8 hours, until the rice has absorbed all the liquid. 3. Then stir in the remaining 2 tablespoons of olive oil. Cover and let rest for 10 minutes. 4. Serve warm. 5. Refrigerate leftovers for up to 1 week, or freeze for up to 3 months.

Quinoa and Brussels Sprouts Casserole

Prep Time: 10 minutes | Cook Time: 5 to 6 hours | Serves: 8

2 cups quinoa, rinsed
1 onion, finely chopped
3 garlic cloves, minced
4 cups roasted vegetable broth
3 cups Brussels sprouts

1 teaspoon dried marjoram leaves
2 tablespoons lemon juice
2 avocados, peeled and sliced
½ cup pomegranate seeds
1 cup broken walnuts

1. Combine the quinoa, garlic, onion, vegetable broth, marjoram, Brussels sprouts, and lemon juice in the slow cooker. Cover and cook on low for 5 to 6 hours, or until the quinoa is tender. 2. Spread the avocados, pomegranate seeds, and walnuts on top. Serve.

Cheese Veggie Lasagna

Prep Time: 15 minutes | Cook Time: 5½ hours | Serves: 6

2 tablespoons extra-virgin olive oil
1 pound cremini mushrooms, chopped
1 medium yellow onion, chopped
1 cup finely chopped peeled zucchini or yellow squash
½ teaspoon sea salt
3 to 4½ cups red pasta sauce (depending on how saucy you want it to be), divided

8 to 10 thick lasagna noodles
1 (24-ounce) container 2 percent small-curd cottage cheese, divided
2 cups shredded mozzarella or provolone cheese, divided
2 (10-ounce) bags frozen chopped spinach, divided
1 teaspoon Italian seasoning
Grated Parmesan, pesto, or chopped fresh parsley, for topping (optional)

1. Coat the slow cooker with the olive oil. 2. Add in the onion, mushrooms, zucchini, and salt. Cook over high heat, stirring frequently, for 3 to 4 minutes, until vegetables begin to sizzle. Pour into a large bowl. 3. Turn the heat to low and pour half of the pasta sauce into the slow cooker in an even layer. 4. Top sauce with two whole lasagna noodles, breaking one-third of the noodles in half to fill in the sides, if desired. 5. Sprinkle one-third of the cottage cheese over the noodles, then sprinkle with 1 cup of the vegetable mixture, ⅔ cup of the mozzarella cheese, and a thin layer of the frozen spinach. 6. Repeat with remaining cottage cheese, vegetable mixture and frozen spinach. 7. Finish with a drizzle of the remaining tomato sauce and a sprinkle of Italian seasoning. 8. Cover and cook on low for 5 hours, until the noodles are cooked and the lasagna is heated through. 9. Then sprinkle the remaining 1⅓ cups of mozzarella cheese on top. Cover and cook for 30 minutes more, until the cheese has melted and is bubbly. 10. Let the lasagna rest for 1 hour before serving. If you prefer a thinner, soup-like lasagna, serve immediately. 11. Top with grated Parmesan, pesto, or parsley (if using). Serve warm. 12. Refrigerate leftovers for up to 1 week, or freeze for up to 2 months.

Cheese Chili Mac

Prep Time: 10 minutes | Cook Time: 7 to 8 hours | Serves: 8

Nonstick cooking spray, for coating the slow cooker
5 tablespoons minced garlic
3 (15-ounce) cans beans of your choice (pinto, kidney, black, navy, etc.)
3 cups canned diced tomatoes, drained
1 small yellow onion, diced
4 cups savory vegetable broth or store-bought vegetable broth
½ teaspoon sea salt

½ teaspoon ground black pepper
2 teaspoons chili powder
1 teaspoon paprika
2 tablespoons ground cumin
½ teaspoon cayenne pepper
8 ounces whole-grain macaroni
8 ounces shredded mild Cheddar cheese
8 ounces shredded Colby-Jack cheese

1. Coat the bottom and sides of the slow cooker with cooking spray. 2. Set the heat to high and add the garlic; cook for 2 to 3 minutes, until fragrant. 3. Stir in the beans, onion, tomatoes, broth, salt, black pepper, paprika, chili powder, cumin, and cayenne. Cover and reduce the heat to low; cook for 7 hours until the beans are easily mashed. 4. Then add the macaroni and stir to mix well. Cover and cook for 20 to 30 minutes longer, until the macaroni is soft. 5. Add the Cheddar cheese and Colby-Jack cheese. Cover and cook for 5 to 10 minutes more, until the cheese starts to melt. 6. Serve the chili mac warm. 7. Refrigerate leftovers for up to 1 week, or freeze for up to 3 months.

Slow-Cooked Bell Peppers

Prep Time: 20 minutes | Cook Time: 5 to 6 hours | Serves: 8

8 to 10 bell peppers of different colors, stemmed, seeded, and halved
1 red onion, chopped

1 tablespoon olive oil
1 teaspoon dried thyme leaves

1. Place the bell pepper in a slow cooker. Drizzle with the olive oil and spread the red onion and thyme on top. 2. Cover and cook on low for 5 to 6 hours, stirring once if desired, until the peppers are tender and slightly browned on the edges. Serve.

Curried Butternut Squash

Prep Time: 20 minutes | Cook Time: 6 to 7 hours | Serves: 8

1 large butternut squash, peeled, seeded, and cut into 1-inch pieces
3 acorn squash, peeled, seeded, and cut into 1-inch pieces
2 onions, finely chopped
5 garlic cloves, minced

1 tablespoon curry powder
⅓ cup freshly squeezed orange juice
½ teaspoon salt

1. Combine all of the ingredients in the slow cooker. 2. Cover and cook on low for 6 to 7 hours, or until the squash is tender when pierced with a fork. 3. Serve warm.

Summer Succotash

Prep Time: 20 minutes | Cook Time: 8 to 9 hours | Serves: 10

2 cups dry lima beans, rinsed and drained
4 cups frozen corn
1 red onion, minced
4 large tomatoes, seeded and chopped

5 cups roasted vegetable broth
1 teaspoon dried thyme leaves
1 teaspoon dried basil leaves
1 bay leaf

1. Combine all of the ingredients in the slow cooker. 2. Cover and cook on low for 8 to 9 hours, or until the lima beans are tender. 3. Remove and discard the bay leaf. Serve warm.

Garlic Sweet Potatoes & Onions

Prep Time: 20 minutes | Cook Time: 7 to 8 hours | Serves: 8

5 large sweet potatoes, peeled and chopped
3 onions, chopped
5 garlic cloves, minced
2 jalapeño or habanero peppers, minced
2 tablespoons olive oil

⅓ cup roasted vegetable broth
1 tablespoon chili powder
1 teaspoon ground cumin
½ teaspoon salt

1. Combine all of the ingredients in the slow cooker. Cover and cook on low for 7 to 8 hours. 2. Stir the mixture gently and serve.

Garlic Carrots and Parsnips

Prep Time: 20 minutes | Cook Time: 5 to 7 hours | Serves: 8

6 large carrots, peeled and cut into 2-inch pieces
5 large parsnips, peeled and cut into 2-inch pieces
2 red onions, chopped
4 garlic cloves, minced

2 tablespoons olive oil
1 tablespoon honey
½ teaspoon salt

1. Add all ingredients to the slow cooker and stir gently. 2. Cover and cook on low for 5 to 7 hours, or until the vegetables are tender. Serve warm.

Curry Legume Dal

Prep Time: 15 minutes | Cook Time: 6 to 8 hours | Serves: 4

2 cups dried black, red, and green lentils, soaked overnight and drained
5 cups water
1 large tomato, diced
1 onion, diced
5 garlic cloves, minced

1 tablespoon ground cumin
1 teaspoon ground ginger
1 teaspoon ground turmeric
1 teaspoon curry powder
1 teaspoon salt
½ teaspoon freshly ground black pepper

1. Add all the ingredients to the slow cooker and mix well. 2. Cover and cook on low for 6 to 8 hours. Serve warm.

Lentils and Butternut Squash Stew

Prep Time: 15 minutes | Cook Time: 6 to 8 hours | Serves: 4

1½ cups red and/or green lentils, soaked overnight and drained
8 ounces butternut squash, diced
4 cups water
1 (15-ounce) can diced tomatoes, with their juice
1 cup full-fat coconut milk
1 teaspoon ghee (optional)
1 onion, chopped

2 garlic cloves, minced
2 teaspoons ground cumin
1 teaspoon chili powder
1 teaspoon salt
½ teaspoon freshly ground black pepper
2 scallions, sliced, for garnish

1. Add all the ingredients to the slow cooker and mix well. 2. Cover and cook low 6 to 8 hours. 3. Sprinkle with the scallions and serve warm.

Aromatic Beans Stew

Prep Time: 20 minutes | Cook Time: 3 to 3½ hours | Serves: 10

1½ pounds green beans
3 cups fresh soybeans
3 bulbs fennel, cored and chopped
1 jalapeño pepper, minced
1 lemongrass stalk

½ cup canned coconut milk
2 tablespoons lime juice
½ teaspoon salt
⅓ cup chopped fresh cilantro

1. Combine the green beans, soybeans, jalapeño pepper, fennel, lemongrass, lime juice, coconut milk, and salt in the slow cooker. Stir until well combined. 2. Cover and cook on low for 3 to 3½ hours, or until the vegetables are tender. 3. Once done, remove and discard the lemongrass. 4. Sprinkle with cilantro and serve.

Lentil Summer Veggie Stew

Prep Time: 10 minutes | Cook Time: 6 to 7 hours | Serves: 4

1 cup dried brown lentils, picked over and rinsed
1 small sweet onion, finely chopped
1 tablespoon minced garlic
2 teaspoons dried oregano
1 teaspoon ground cinnamon
2 small zucchinis, chopped
1 medium yellow squash, chopped

1 tablespoon tomato paste
½ teaspoon kosher salt
¼ teaspoon freshly ground black pepper
2½ cups no-salt-added vegetable broth
½ cup unsweetened pomegranate juice
Chopped fresh basil, for garnish (optional)

1. Combine the lentils, garlic, onion, zucchini, yellow squash, oregano, cinnamon, salt, pepper, tomato paste, broth, and juice in the slow cooker. Gently toss well. 2. Cover and cook on low for 6 to 7 hours, until the lentils are soft. 3. Garnish with basil (if using) and serve immediately. 4. Refrigerate leftovers for up to 5 days or freeze for up to 6 months.

Tasty Butternut Squash Chili

Prep Time: 15 minutes | Cook Time: 5 to 7 hours | Serves: 8

1 medium sweet onion, finely chopped
2 poblano peppers, finely chopped
2 tablespoons minced garlic
1 (2- to 3-pound) butternut squash, cut into 1-inch cubes
2 (15- to 16-ounce) cans no-salt-added small red beans or kidney
beans, drained and rinsed
1 (28-ounce) can no-salt-added crushed tomatoes, with their juices

3 cups no-salt-added vegetable broth
1 (10-ounce) bag frozen corn
1 tablespoon chili powder
1 teaspoon dried oregano
½ teaspoon kosher salt
Freshly ground pepper
Chopped fresh cilantro, for garnish (optional)

1. Add the onion, squash, beans, poblano peppers, garlic, tomatoes with their juices, corn, broth, chili powder, oregano, and salt to the slow cooker. Stir to mix well. 2. Cover and cook on low for 5 to 7 hours, until the squash is fork-tender. 3. Season with black pepper and top with cilantro (if using). Serve warm. 4. Refrigerate leftovers for up to 4 days or freeze for up to 2 months.

Thai Curried Sweet Potato Soup with Cashews

Prep Time: 15 minutes | Cook Time: 5 to 6 hours | Serves: 6

1 small yellow onion, finely chopped
2 tablespoons coconut aminos
1 tablespoon light brown sugar
2 tablespoons Thai red curry paste
3 cups no-salt-added vegetable broth

2½ pounds sweet potatoes, peeled and cut into 1-inch pieces
1 (13- to 14-ounce) can coconut milk
Chopped fresh basil, for garnish
¼ cup toasted cashews, for garnish

1. Combine the onion, brown sugar, coconut aminos, curry paste, and broth in the slow cooker. Add in the sweet potatoes and stir well. 2. Cover and cook on low for 5 to 6 hours, until the sweet potatoes are tender. Pour in the coconut milk and allow the mixture to cool slightly. 3. Pour soup in batches into a food processor and puree. 4. Pour soup into serving bowls and garnish with basil and cashews. 5. Refrigerate leftovers for up to 5 days or freeze for up to 3 months.

Creamy Cauliflower & Sweet Potato Soup

Prep Time: 10 minutes | Cook Time: 6 to 8 hours | Serves: 6

1 head cauliflower, trimmed and chopped
2 pounds sweet potatoes, peeled and chopped
1 onion, diced
3 garlic cloves, minced
½ cup chopped fresh cilantro
1 (15-ounce) can diced tomatoes, with their juice
1 (15-ounce) can coconut cream or full-fat coconut milk

2 teaspoons ground cumin
1 teaspoon ground ginger
1 teaspoon curry powder or garam masala
1 teaspoon salt
1 teaspoon ground turmeric
½ teaspoon freshly ground black pepper

1. Combine all the ingredients in the slow cooker and stir to mix well. 2. Cover and cook on low for 6 to 8 hours. Serve warm.

Curried Coconut Chickpeas

Prep Time: 15 minutes | Cook Time: 6 to 8 hours | Serves: 4

2 (15-ounce) cans chickpeas, rinsed and drained
1 (15-ounce) can full-fat coconut milk or coconut cream
Juice of 1 lime
8 ounces Roma tomatoes, diced
1 small onion, diced
2 garlic cloves, minced

1 tablespoon Thai red curry paste
1 teaspoon curry powder
1 teaspoon ground cumin
½ teaspoon salt
¼ teaspoon freshly ground black pepper

1. Combine all the ingredients in the slow cooker and stir to mix well. 2. Cover and cook on low for 6 to 8 hours. Serve warm.

Cheese Farro Risotto

Prep Time: 15 minutes | Cook Time: 4 hours | Serves: 4

Nonstick cooking spray
2¼ cups vegetable broth
1 cup whole farro
1 medium yellow onion, finely diced
1 tablespoon unsalted butter
1 teaspoon garlic powder

3 carrots, peeled and grated
½ teaspoon salt, plus more for seasoning
4 ounces goat cheese, crumbled
¼ cup boiling water, if needed
Freshly ground black pepper

1. Lightly spray the slow cooker with nonstick cooking spray. Pour in the vegetable broth. 2. Combine the farro, butter, onion, and garlic powder in a microwave-safe bowl. Microwave on high heat for 5 minutes, stirring once halfway through. Then add the mixture to the slow cooker and stir in the carrots and salt. 3. Cover and cook on low for 4 hours. 4. Pour up to ¼ cup of boiling water to the slow cooker to loosen the mixture if needed. 5. Spread the goat cheese on the risotto. Season with more salt and pepper if desired. Serve.

Lime Lentil & Bean Salad

Prep Time: 10 minutes | Cook Time: 4 hours | Serves: 2

1 cup vegetable broth
1 (15-ounce) can pinto beans, rinsed and drained
⅔ cup brown lentils
3 tablespoons fresh lime juice, divided
1 teaspoon garlic powder
¼ teaspoon dried oregano

½ teaspoon salt, plus more for seasoning
6 ounces cherry tomatoes, halved
2 teaspoons olive oil
1 ounce queso fresco, crumbled
Freshly ground black pepper

1. In the slow cooker, combine the vegetable broth, lentils, beans, 1 tablespoon of lime juice, oregano, garlic powder, and salt. 2. Cover and cook on low for 4 hours. 3. Then add in the remaining 2 tablespoons of lime juice, olive oil, cherry tomatoes, and queso fresco. Stir to mix well. 4. Season with more salt and pepper if desired. Serve.

Savory Ratatouille

Prep Time: 15 minutes | Cook Time: 5 hours | Serves: 4

1 medium yellow onion, diced
2 tablespoons olive oil, divided
1 tablespoon tomato paste
2 teaspoons garlic powder
1 teaspoon dried basil
¼ teaspoon salt, plus more for seasoning

8 ounces eggplant, cut into 1-inch dice
8 ounces zucchini, cut into 1-inch dice
1 large red, yellow, or orange bell pepper, seeded and cut into 1-inch pieces
Freshly ground black pepper

1. In a microwave-safe bowl, combine 1 tablespoon of olive oil and onion. Cover and microwave on high for 5 minutes, stirring once halfway through. 2. Add in the tomato paste, basil, salt, garlic powder, and the remaining olive oil. Stir to mix well and pour the mixture into the slow cooker. 3. Then stir in the zucchini, eggplant, and bell pepper. 4. Cover and cook on low for 5 hours. 5. Season with more salt and pepper if needed, and serve.

Hot Burrito Bowls

Prep Time: 15 minutes | Cook Time: 7 to 8 hours | Serves: 6

2 (15-ounce) cans black beans, drained and rinsed
2 cups cubed sweet potato
1 (14.5-ounce) can no-salt-added diced tomatoes
1 cup savory vegetable broth or low-sodium vegetable broth
1 cup chopped onion
1 bell pepper, chopped
½ cup frozen corn

½ cup spicy salsa
1 tablespoon hot sauce (or to taste)
1 teaspoon smoked paprika
½ teaspoon ground cumin
Freshly ground black pepper
Sliced avocado, radish, cilantro, and/or lime, for garnish (optional)

1. Combine all the ingredients in the slow cooker. Cover and cook on low for 7 to 8 hours or until the vegetables are tender. 2. Serve with your favorite toppings.

Spicy Black Bean Enchiladas

Prep Time: 15 minutes | Cook Time: 6 to 8 hours | Serves: 6

2 (14.5-ounce) cans black beans, drained and rinsed
1 (14.5-ounce) can fire-roasted tomatoes with garlic drained and juice reserved
1 cup frozen corn kernels
1 bell pepper (any color), chopped
1 onion, chopped

1 (4-ounce) can green chiles
1 cup low-fat shredded Mexican cheese blend, divided
2 teaspoons ground cumin
Nonstick cooking spray
2 cups spicy salsa, divided
12 (6-inch) corn tortillas

1. In a large bowl, gently mash the beans with a fork. Add the corn, tomatoes, onion, bell pepper, ½ cup of cheese, chiles, and cumin to the bowl and stir until well combined. 2. Spray the slow cooker with cooking spray. Spread 1 cup of salsa in the slow cooker to evenly coat the bottom. 3. Divide the bean filling evenly among each tortilla and roll them up tight. Arrange 6 enchiladas in a single layer in the bottom of the slow cooker, seam-side down. Top with ½ cup of salsa and sprinkle with ¼ cup of cheese. 4. Place the remaining 6 enchiladas seam-side down to create a second layer. Then spread the remaining ½ cup of salsa and ¼ cup of cheese on top. 5. Cover and cook on low for 6 to 8 hours. 6. Serve with your favorite toppings.

Chapter 3 Poultry

Tender Spiced Turkey Breast

Prep Time: 10 minutes | Cook Time: 8 hours | Serves: 6

1 tablespoon olive oil
2 teaspoons smoked paprika
1 teaspoon brown sugar
1 teaspoon dried sage
½ teaspoon chili powder

½ teaspoon garlic powder
½ teaspoon onion powder
½ teaspoon salt
½ teaspoon freshly ground black pepper
1 (2-pound) bone-in turkey breast half, skin removed

1. In a small bowl, whisk together the olive oil, paprika, brown sugar, sage, chili powder, garlic powder, onion powder, salt, and pepper. Place the turkey on a large sheet of aluminum foil. Rub the oil mixture all over the turkey. Loosely wrap the turkey in the foil and place it in the slow cooker. 2. Cover and cook on low for 8 hours, or until the temperature at the thickest part of the breast registers 165°F. 3. Gently open the foil, being careful of the steam. Transfer the turkey to a cutting board. Loosely tent the turkey with foil and allow it to rest for 10 minutes. 4. Slice the turkey and serve.

Italian Turkey Meatloaf with Baked Potatoes

Prep Time: 10 minutes | Cook Time: 8 hours | Serves: 4

1 pound ground turkey
1 (8-ounce) can tomato sauce
1 cup Italian-style bread crumbs
½ cup finely diced yellow onion

1 teaspoon salt
¼ teaspoon freshly ground black pepper
4 russet potatoes

1. Combine the turkey, tomato sauce, bread crumbs, onion, salt, and pepper in a large bowl. Mix with your hands to combine thoroughly. Arrange the meatloaf mixture in a loaf pan that fits inside your slow cooker insert. Shape the mixture into a loaf, leaving some room between the loaf and the pan sides for melted fat to collect. Cover the top of the pan with aluminum foil. Place the pan in the slow cooker. 2. Scrub the potatoes and pierce each potato with a fork several times. Wrap the potatoes in foil. Place the potatoes around the loaf pan. You may need to stack them to fit or even balance them on the sides of the loaf pan. 3. Cover and cook on low for 8 hours. 4. When cooking is finished, transfer the loaf pan to a wire rack, remove the foil, and allow it to sit for 5 minutes. Slice and serve with the baked potatoes.

Cheesy Turkey Meatballs

Prep Time: 15 minutes | Cook Time: 5 hours | Serves: 4

1 pound lean ground turkey
1 large egg, lightly beaten
½ cup bread crumbs
1 teaspoon chili powder
1 teaspoon salt

½ teaspoon garlic powder
½ teaspoon onion powder
1 (28-ounce) jar all-natural or organic spaghetti sauce
1 cup shredded mozzarella cheese
Cooked spaghetti, for serving (optional)

1. Combine the turkey, egg, bread crumbs, salt, garlic powder, chili powder, and onion powder in a large bowl, and mix with clean hands to combine fully. Form the mixture into 1-inch meatballs. Arrange the meatballs in the slow cooker. Pour the spaghetti sauce over the meatballs. 2. Cover and cook on low for 5 hours. 3. Remove the lid and sprinkle the mozzarella cheese on top of the meatballs and sauce. Cook for about 10 minutes on high heat without the lid until the cheese is melted. 4. Carefully scoop the meatballs and sauce onto serving plates—over spaghetti, if desired.

Delicious Rosemary Lemon Chicken with Vegetables

Prep Time: 10 minutes | Cook Time: 7-8 hours | Serves: 6

1 pound baby potatoes, halved
6 medium carrots, peeled and sliced
2 medium onions, sliced
Freshly ground black pepper
3 teaspoons dried rosemary, divided

2 pounds boneless, skinless chicken breasts
Juice of 2 lemons (about ½ cup)
1 cup low-sodium chicken broth
4 fresh rosemary sprigs
4 garlic cloves, minced

1. Place the potatoes, carrots, and onions in the bottom of the slow cooker. Sprinkle them with the black pepper and 1½ teaspoons of dried rosemary. Place the chicken on top of the vegetables. 2. Pour the lemon juice and stock over the chicken and vegetables. Place the fresh rosemary and garlic on top of the chicken. Cover and cook on low for 7 to 8 hours, until the chicken is cooked through and vegetables are tender. 3. When cooking is finished, remove and discard the rosemary sprigs. Serve hot.

Classic Chicken Cacciatore

Prep Time: 10 minutes | Cook Time: 7-8 hours | Serves: 6

4 portobello mushrooms, stemmed, thinly sliced
1 cup sliced button mushrooms
1 (28-ounce) can no-salt-added diced tomatoes
1 (6-ounce) can tomato paste
2 bell peppers (any color), thinly sliced
1 onion, diced

4 garlic cloves, minced
2 teaspoons dried basil
2 teaspoons dried oregano
Freshly ground black pepper
2 pounds boneless, skinless chicken breasts or thighs

1. Put the mushrooms, tomatoes, tomato paste, bell peppers, onion, garlic, basil, oregano, and black pepper in a 6-quart slow cooker. Stir to mix well. Add the chicken and mix again. Cover and cook on low for 7 to 8 hours, until the chicken is cooked through and the vegetables are tender. 2. When cooking is finished, serve hot, over couscous, quinoa, mashed potatoes, riced cauliflower, or whole-wheat pasta, if desired.

Nutritious Chicken Spaghetti with Peppers and Onions

Prep Time: 10 minutes | Cook Time: 7-8 hours | Serves: 6

Nonstick cooking spray
1½ pounds boneless, skinless chicken breasts (about 6 breasts)
1 green bell pepper, sliced
1 onion, halved and sliced
1 (28-ounce) can crushed tomatoes
1 (14-ounce) can no-salt-added diced tomatoes

4 garlic cloves, minced
1 tablespoon balsamic vinegar
1 teaspoon dried oregano
1 teaspoon Italian seasoning
12 ounces whole-wheat spaghetti

1. Spray a 6-quart slow cooker with the cooking spray. Place the chicken breasts in the bottom and top them with the sliced bell pepper and onion. 2. Mix together the crushed tomatoes, diced tomatoes, garlic, vinegar, oregano, and Italian seasoning in a large bowl. Pour this over the chicken and vegetables. 3. Cover and cook on high for 4 hours or on low for 7 to 8 hours. 4. Before serving, cook the pasta according to the package directions, omitting the salt and any fat. Serve the chicken and sauce on top of the cooked pasta.

Herbed Marinara-Braised Turkey Meatball

Prep Time: 15 minutes | Cook Time: 6 hours | Serves: 6

3 tablespoons extra-virgin olive oil
1 pound ground turkey
1 pound breakfast sausage, crumbled
½ cup almond flour
1 egg
1 tablespoon chopped basil

2 teaspoons chopped oregano
½ teaspoon salt
¼ teaspoon freshly ground black pepper
2 cups simple marinara sauce
1 cup shredded mozzarella cheese

1. Lightly grease the insert of the slow cooker with 1 tablespoon of the olive oil. 2. In a large bowl, mix together the turkey, sausage, egg, basil, almond flour, oregano, salt, and pepper. roll the mixture into golf ball–sized meatballs. 3. In a large skillet over medium-high heat, heat the remaining 2 tablespoons of the olive oil. Add the meatballs and brown for 7 minutes, turning several times. 4. Transfer the meatballs to the insert and add the marinara sauce. 5. Cover and cook on low for 6 hours. 6. Serve topped with the mozzarella cheese.

Creamy Turkey-Pumpkin Ragout

Prep Time: 15 minutes | Cook Time: 8 hours | Serves: 6

1 tablespoon extra-virgin olive oil
1 pound boneless turkey thighs, cut into 1½-inch chunks
3 cups cubed pumpkin, cut into 1-inch chunks
1 red bell pepper, diced
½ sweet onion, cut in half and sliced
1 tablespoon minced garlic
1½ cups chicken broth

1½ cups coconut milk
2 teaspoons chopped fresh thyme
½ cup coconut cream
Salt, for seasoning
Freshly ground black pepper, for seasoning
12 slices cooked bacon, chopped, for garnish

1. Lightly grease the insert of the slow cooker with the olive oil. 2. Add the turkey, pumpkin, red bell pepper, onion, garlic, broth, coconut milk, and thyme. 3. Cover and cook on low for 8 hours. 4. Stir in the coconut cream and season with the salt and pepper. 5. Serve topped with the bacon.

Herbed Turkey and Mushroom Wild Rice Casserole

Prep Time: 15 minutes | Cook Time: 7-8 hours | Serves: 8

Nonstick cooking spray
1 cup cold low-fat or fat-free milk, or plant-based milk
3 tablespoons extra-virgin olive oil
3 tablespoons cornstarch
6 cups low-sodium turkey broth, divided
2 pounds turkey breast tenderloin, cut into ¾-inch pieces
2 cups wild rice, rinsed and drained
1 onion, chopped

1 cup sliced carrot
1 cup sliced celery
1 cup sliced button mushrooms
1 teaspoon dried tarragon
¼ teaspoon freshly ground black pepper
½ cup sliced almonds
½ cup chopped scallions, for garnish (optional)

1. Grease the inside of a 6-quart slow cooker with the cooking spray. 2. In a small bowl, whisk together the cold milk, olive oil, and cornstarch. Add 1 cup of broth and toss to combine. Pour this mixture into the slow cooker. 3. Add the turkey, rice, onion, carrot, celery, mushrooms, tarragon, and black pepper to the slow cooker. Add in the remaining 5 cups of broth and stir to combine. Cover and cook on low for 7 to 8 hours, until vegetables are tender, the rice has absorbed the liquid, and the turkey is cooked through. 4. When cooking is finished, serve hot, garnished with the sliced almonds and scallions, if using.

Lemony Spicy White Chicken Chili

Prep Time: 15 minutes | Cook Time: 8 hours | Serves: 7

1½ pounds boneless, skinless chicken breasts
4 cups chicken stock or vegetable broth
2 (14-ounce) cans no-salt-added cannellini beans, drained and rinsed
2 cups frozen corn
2 green bell peppers, chopped
3 jalapeño peppers, seeded, membranes removed, minced
1 onion, chopped
1 (4-ounce) can diced green chiles
4 garlic cloves, minced

2 teaspoons ground cumin
1 teaspoon chili powder
1 teaspoon dried oregano
½ teaspoon salt
¼ teaspoon cayenne pepper
¼ cup yellow cornmeal
¼ cup fat-free or low-fat milk, or plant-based milk
1 cup chopped cilantro
1 lime, cut into wedges

1. Place the chicken, stock, beans, corn, bell peppers, jalapeños, onion, chiles, garlic, cumin, chili powder, oregano, salt, and cayenne pepper in a 6-quart slow cooker. Cover and cook on high for 4 hours or on low for 8 hours. 2. Just prior to serving, mix together the cornmeal and milk in a small bowl. Stir this into the slow cooker and allow the sauce to thicken slightly, about 5 minutes. 3. Serve hot, topped with the cilantro and a squeeze of lime juice.

Tasty Fontina-Stuffed Turkey Meatballs in Sauce

Prep Time: 20 minutes | Cook Time: 7 hours | Serves: 8

For the Sauce:
¼ cup (½ stick) unsalted butter, melted
1 (14.5-ounce) can crushed tomatoes
1 tablespoon extra-virgin olive oil
2 garlic cloves, minced
2 teaspoons dried basil
For the Meatballs:
2 large eggs
2 cups riced cauliflower
½ cup almond meal
2 cups grated Parmesan cheese, divided
2 tablespoons Italian seasoning
1 teaspoon kosher salt

1 teaspoon dried parsley
1 teaspoon kosher salt
½ teaspoon freshly ground black pepper
1 cup heavy (whipping) cream

½ teaspoon freshly ground black pepper
½ teaspoon garlic powder
12 ounces ground turkey
1 pound Italian sausage, casings removed
8 ounces fontina cheese, cut into 24 cubes

1. To make the sauce: In the slow cooker, stir together the butter, tomatoes, olive oil, garlic, basil, parsley, salt, and pepper. 2. To make the meatballs: In a large bowl, beat the eggs, then whisk in the cauliflower rice, almond meal, pepper, 1 cup of Parmesan cheese, salt, Italian seasoning, and garlic powder. 3. Add the turkey and sausage and mix to combine. Form the mixture into 24 (1-inch) balls. 4. Stuff a cheese cube into the center of each meatball and press the meat mixture around it so it is fully encased. Place the stuffed meatballs in the slow cooker. Cover and cook for 7 hours on low. 5. Just before serving, stir the heavy cream into the sauce. Serve hot, garnished with the remaining 1 cup of Parmesan cheese.

Easy Juicy "Roasted" Duck

Prep Time: 15 minutes | Cook Time: 7-8 hours | Serves: 8

3 tablespoons extra-virgin olive oil, divided
1 (2½-pound) whole duck, giblets removed
Salt, for seasoning
Freshly ground black pepper, for seasoning
4 garlic cloves, crushed

6 thyme sprigs, chopped
1 cinnamon stick, broken into several pieces
1 sweet onion, coarsely chopped
¼ cup chicken broth

1. Lightly grease the insert of the slow cooker with 1 tablespoon of the olive oil. 2. Rub the remaining 2 tablespoons of the olive oil all over the duck and season with the salt and pepper. stuff the garlic, thyme, and cinnamon into the cavity of the duck. 3. Place the onion on the bottom of the slow cooker and place the duck on top so it does not touch the bottom of the insert, and pour in the broth. 4. Cover and cook on low for 7 to 8 hours, or until the internal temperature reaches 180°f on an instant-read thermometer. 5. Serve warm.

Homemade Caribbean-Style Jerk Chicken

Prep Time: 30 minutes | Cook Time: 6 hours | Serves: 8

1 (14-ounce) can coconut milk
¼ cup coconut oil
Juice of 1 lime
2 tablespoons blackstrap molasses
8 scallions, coarsely chopped
3 garlic cloves, peeled
2 habanero peppers, halved and seeded

1 (1-inch) fresh ginger, peeled and roughly chopped
1 tablespoon fresh thyme
2 teaspoons ground allspice
1 teaspoon kosher salt
¼ teaspoon ground cardamom
2 pounds boneless, skinless chicken thighs
Lime wedges, for garnish

1. In a food processor or blender, mix the coconut milk, coconut oil, lime juice, molasses, scallions, garlic, habaneros, ginger, thyme, allspice, salt, and cardamom. Process to combine well. 2. Put the chicken in the slow cooker and pour in the sauce. Toss to coat the chicken evenly with the sauce. Cover and cook for 6 hours on low. Serve hot, garnished with lime wedges.

Tangy Bacon-Wrapped Chicken with Barbecue Sauce

Prep Time: 15 minutes | Cook Time: 8 hours | Serves: 4

12 bacon slices
4 large boneless, skinless chicken thighs
3 tablespoons red wine vinegar
3 tablespoons chicken broth
3 tablespoons tomato paste
3 tablespoons prepared mustard
2 tablespoons unsalted butter, melted

2 teaspoons soy sauce or tamari
1 teaspoon fish sauce or additional soy sauce or tamari
3 tablespoons erythritol or ¼ teaspoon stevia powder
2 teaspoons chili powder
1 teaspoon ground cumin
½ teaspoon cayenne pepper
½ onion, diced

1. Wrap 3 pieces of bacon around each chicken thigh. Arrange the wrapped chicken in the slow cooker in a single layer. 2. In a medium bowl, whisk together the red wine vinegar, chicken broth, tomato paste, mustard, butter, soy sauce, fish sauce, erythritol, chili powder, cumin, and cayenne. Stir in the onion. Pour the mixture over the chicken. Cover and cook for 8 hours on low. Serve hot.

Basil Chicken Meatballs in Italian Tomato Sauce

Prep Time: 5 minutes | Cook Time: 3-6 hours | Serves: 4

12 frozen chicken meatballs
1 tablespoon vegetable oil
2 cloves garlic, minced
1½ tablespoons minced basil

1 medium onion, minced
2 (15-ounce) cans fire-roasted tomatoes, undrained
1 teaspoon crushed red pepper flakes
1 teaspoon kosher salt

1. Defrost the meatballs according to package instructions. 2. Meanwhile, pour oil into a 4-quart slow cooker. Add garlic and set cooker on high. Stir continuously until garlic becomes very fragrant, 2–3 minutes. 3. Add the remaining ingredients except salt. Stir. Cook on low for 3–6 hours. Stir in the salt and taste; add more salt if needed.

Tender Chicken with Potatoes, Parsnips, and Onions

Prep Time: 10 minutes | Cook Time: 8 hours | Serves: 6

4 medium onions, sliced
1 whole roasting chicken (5 or more pounds)
6 large red-skin potatoes, halved

4 parsnips, diced
1 teaspoon kosher salt
½ teaspoon black pepper

1. Cover the bottom of a 6- to 7-quart slow cooker with half of the onions. 2. Place the chicken, breast side up, on top of the onions. 3. Cover the chicken with the remaining onions. 4. Arrange the potatoes and parsnips around the chicken. 5. Cover and cook on low for 8 hours or until the chicken has an internal temperature of 165°F as measured using a food thermometer. Discard the chicken skin. Sprinkle the salt and pepper evenly on top of the chicken and vegetables before serving.

Traditional Tuscan Chicken

Prep Time: 2 minutes | Cook Time: 4 hours | Serves: 4

1 pound boneless, skinless chicken breasts
4 cloves garlic, minced
1 shallot, minced
2 tablespoons white wine vinegar

1 tablespoon lemon juice
1 tablespoon minced fresh rosemary
1 cup Chicken Stock

1. Place all ingredients into a 4-quart slow cooker. Stir. Cook on low for 4 hours or until the chicken is fully cooked. 2. When cooking is finished, serve.

South African–Style Chicken Breasts

Prep Time: 10 minutes | Cook Time: 8 hours | Serves: 6

Cooking spray
6 boneless, skinless chicken breasts
½ cup barbecue sauce
½ cup chicken broth
1 medium onion, diced
½ cup dried apricots, halved

½ cup golden raisins
1 tablespoon curry powder
1 teaspoon coriander
½ teaspoon ground cinnamon
2 garlic cloves, minced
3 cups cooked couscous

1. Lightly spray inside of a 4-quart slow cooker with cooking spray. Place chicken in slow cooker in a single layer, overlapping to fit if necessary. 2. Combine the remaining ingredients except the couscous, and pour over chicken in a medium bowl. Cover and cook on low for 8 hours. 3. Serve over couscous.

Classic Basque-Style Chicken

Prep Time: 10 minutes | Cook Time: 7-8 hours | Serves: 6

Cooking spray
2 tablespoons vegetable oil
2 medium onions, peeled and thinly sliced into rings
2 cloves garlic, peeled and minced
1 large red bell pepper, seeded and cut into ½"-thick strips
1 yellow, green, or orange bell pepper, seeded and cut into ½"-thick strips
1 teaspoon smoked paprika
1 teaspoon dried thyme
1 chicken, cut into eighths

2 tablespoons red wine vinegar
½ cup Chicken Stock
1 (12-ounce) package chorizo-style sausages, cut into ¼" slices
1 (15-ounce) can diced tomatoes, drained
¼ teaspoon cayenne pepper (optional)
1 teaspoon kosher salt, if needed
¼ teaspoon black pepper, if needed
3 cups cooked rice
¼ cup parsley leaves, chopped (for garnish)

1. Lightly grease the inside of a 6-quart slow cooker with cooking spray. 2. Heat the oil in a large skillet over medium-high heat. Add the onions, garlic, bell peppers, paprika, and thyme to skillet and sauté frequently until vegetables soften, 7–8 minutes. 3. Transfer the vegetables to the slow cooker. Return the skillet to the stovetop and add the chicken. Lightly brown the chicken, about 2 minutes per side (chicken will not be cooked through). 4. Place the chicken over the vegetables in the slow cooker. Stir in the wine vinegar, broth, chorizo, and diced tomatoes. Cover and cook on low for 7–8 hours (or on high for 3–4 hours), until chicken is cooked through and juices run clear when pierced with a knife. 5. Stir in the cayenne pepper, if using. Taste and stir in the salt and pepper, if needed. Serve the chicken over rice. Ladle on sauce and garnish with the parsley.

Crowd-Pleasing Pineapple Teriyaki Drumsticks

Prep Time: 10 minutes | Cook Time: 7-8 hours | Serves: 12

12 chicken drumsticks
1 (8-ounce) can pineapple slices in juice, undrained
¼ cup teriyaki sauce

1 teaspoon ground ginger
¼ cup hoisin sauce

1. Arrange the drumsticks in a single layer on a broiling pan. Broil for 10 minutes on high, flipping the drumsticks once halfway through the cooking time. 2. Drain the juice from the pineapple into a 4- or 6-quart slow cooker, reserving pineapple rings. Add the teriyaki sauce, ginger, and hoisin sauce. Stir to combine. 3.Cut the reserved pineapple rings in half. Add them to the slow cooker. 4. Add the drumsticks to the slow cooker and stir to combine. Cover and cook on low for 4–6 hours. 5. When cooking is finished, serve.

Spicy Vinegary Buffalo Nuggets with Ranch Dressing

Prep Time: 10 minutes | Cook Time: 1 hour | Serves: 6

½ stick (¼ cup) margarine, cut up
1 tablespoon hot sauce, such as Frank's RedHot Sauce
1 tablespoon white vinegar
1 teaspoon garlic powder
1 pound frozen fully cooked chicken nuggets, defrosted
Ranch Dressing
1 cup mayonnaise
½ cup pareve sour cream
½ teaspoon salt

½ teaspoon black pepper
½ teaspoon garlic powder
1½ tablespoons dried parsley
1 tablespoon chopped fresh chives (optional)
1 teaspoon dried dill
¼ teaspoon sweet paprika
1 teaspoon lemon juice
½ teaspoon Worcestershire sauce

1. Place margarine in a small bowl and microwave for 30 seconds, or until almost melted. Remove from microwave and stir until melted completely. 2. Add the hot sauce, vinegar, and garlic powder; stir well. 3. In a 4-quart slow cooker, add about a third of the sauce. Arrange chicken nuggets over sauce. Pour remaining sauce over nuggets. Cover and cook on low for 1 hour. 4. While nuggets are cooking, make the ranch dressing. Stir mayonnaise and sour cream together until completely blended. Stir in remaining dressing ingredients. Chill for at least 30 minutes before serving. 5. Serve the chicken nuggets with the ranch dressing.

Savory Cornish Hens in Plum Sauce

Prep Time: 10 minutes | Cook Time: 4 hours | Serves: 4

Nonstick spray
1 cup Plum Sauce
2 tablespoons soy sauce
1 teaspoon ground ginger

1 teaspoon Chinese five-spice powder
2 Cornish hens
2 green onions, green parts thinly sliced (for garnish)
Toasted sesame seeds (for garnish)

1. Grease the inside of a 6-quart slow cooker with nonstick spray. 2. In a medium bowl, mix the plum sauce, soy sauce, ginger, and five-spice powder. 3. Place hens in the prepared slow cooker, breast side down. Brush with half the plum sauce mixture. Cover and cook on low for 4 hours. 4. Brush with remaining sauce. Re-cover and continue to cook for another 2–4 hours, or until juices run clear when pierced with a knife. 5. Serve the hens garnished with green onions and/or sesame seeds, if desired.

Lemony Chicken with Capers

Prep Time: 15 minutes | Cook Time: 4-6 hours | Serves: 4

2 pounds boneless, skinless chicken legs or thighs
¼ cup freshly squeezed lemon juice
3 tablespoons capers, undrained

1 bay leaf
¾ cup Chicken Stock

1. Arrange the chicken, lemon juice, capers, bay leaf, and stock to a slow cooker. Stir to mix well. 2. Cook on low for 4 to 6 hours or on high for 2 to 3 hours. 3. Remove bay leaf before serving.

Lemony Za'atar Chicken

Prep Time: 5 minutes | Cook Time: 4-6 hours | Serves: 6

2 pounds bone-in, skin-on chicken thighs
2 tablespoons za'atar
⅓ cup water
Juice of 1 lemon
2 teaspoons extra-virgin olive oil
1 teaspoon white vinegar

1 teaspoon dried chopped onion
1 garlic clove, minced
½ teaspoon salt
¼ teaspoon freshly ground black pepper
1 lemon, sliced

1. Add the chicken to a slow cooker. 2. In a small bowl, mix together the za'atar, water, lemon juice, olive oil, vinegar, dried onion, garlic, salt, and pepper. Pour over the chicken in the slow cooker. Top with the lemon slices. 3. Cook on low for 4 to 6 hours or on high for 2 to 3 hours. 4. When cooking is finished, serve.

Unique Thai Chicken Tacos

Prep Time: 10 minutes | Cook Time: 4-6 hours | Serves: 6

2 pounds bone-in, skin-on chicken breasts
1 (15-ounce) can coconut milk
¼ cup chopped fresh cilantro
½ red onion, chopped, divided
3 garlic cloves, minced
1 tablespoon freshly squeezed lime juice
1 teaspoon minced fresh ginger

1 teaspoon turmeric
¾ teaspoon salt
½ teaspoon freshly ground black pepper
8 ounces butter lettuce leaves
Julienned carrots, for garnish
1 serrano pepper, sliced (optional)

1. Add the chicken, coconut milk, cilantro, half of the onion, garlic, salt, lime juice, ginger, turmeric, and black pepper to a slow cooker. Stir to mix well. 2. Cook on low for 4 to 6 hours or on high for 2 to 3 hours. 3.Remove the chicken from the slow cooker and shred the meat using two forks. Place the chicken back into the slow cooker and mix well. 4. Spoon the chicken mixture onto the lettuce leaves with the carrots, peppers (if using), and the remaining onion, wrap, and serve.

Spicy Garlic-Clove Chicken

Prep Time: 10 minutes | Cook Time: 6-8 hours | Serves: 4

2 pounds bone-in, skin-on chicken legs or thighs (or a combination)
40 garlic cloves, peeled
1 cup Chicken Stock
½ small onion, diced

1 teaspoon paprika
½ teaspoon salt
½ teaspoon freshly ground black pepper
1 bay leaf

1. Add the chicken, garlic, stock, onion, paprika, salt, pepper, and bay leaf to a slow cooker. Toss gently to coat the chicken. 2. Cook on low for 6 to 8 hours or on high for 3 to 4 hours. Discard the bay leaf before serving.

Herbed Turkey Meatballs with Spaghetti Squash

Prep Time: 15 minutes | Cook Time: 6 to 7 hours | Serves: 4

1 spaghetti squash, halved lengthwise and seeded
For the Sauce:
1 (15-ounce) can diced tomatoes
½ teaspoon garlic powder
For the Meatballs:
1-pound ground turkey
1 large egg, whisked
½ small white onion, minced
1 teaspoon garlic powder

½ teaspoon dried oregano
½ teaspoon sea salt

½ teaspoon sea salt
½ teaspoon dried oregano
½ teaspoon dried basil leaves
Freshly ground black pepper

1. Place the squash halves in the bottom of the slow cooker, cut-side down. 2. Arrange the diced tomatoes around the squash. 3. Sprinkle with salt, garlic powder and oregano. 4. In a medium bowl, combine the turkey, egg, garlic powder, onion, oregano, salt, basil and pepper. Form the turkey mixture into 12 equal-sized balls, and arrange them in the slow cooker around the spaghetti squash. 5. Cover and cook on low for 6 to 7 hours. 6. Transfer the squash to a work surface and cut it into spaghetti shapes with a fork. 7. Mix the shredded squash with the tomato sauce, top with the meatballs and serve.

Lime-Cilantro Chicken Drumsticks

Prep Time: 15 minutes | Cook Time: 2 to 3 hours | Serves: 4

¼ cup fresh cilantro, chopped
3 tablespoons freshly squeezed lime juice
½ teaspoon garlic powder

½ teaspoon sea salt
¼ teaspoon ground cumin
3 pounds chicken drumsticks

1. In a small bowl, mix together the cilantro, garlic powder, lime juice, salt, and cumin to form a paste. 2. Place the drumsticks in the slow cooker and spread the cilantro paste evenly over each drumstick. 3. Cover and cook on high for 2 to 3 hours, or until the internal temperature of chicken reaches 165°F on a meat thermometer and juices run clear. Serve.

Chimichurri Turkey Breast & Green Beans

Prep Time: 15 minutes | Cook Time: 6 to 7 hours | Serves: 4

1 pound green beans
1 (2-to 3-pound) whole, boneless turkey breast

2 cups chimichurri sauce
½ cup broth of choice

1. Place the green beans in the slow cooker and top with the turkey. Pour in the sauce and broth. 2. Cover and cook on low for 6 to 7 hours, or until the turkey's internal temperature reaches 165°F on a meat thermometer and the juices run clear. Serve.

Balsamic Turkey Wings

Prep Time: 15 minutes | Cook Time: 7 to 8 hours | Serves: 4

1¼ cups balsamic vinegar
2 tablespoons raw honey

1 teaspoon garlic powder
2 pounds turkey wings

1. Whisk the honey, vinegar and garlic powder in a small bowl. 2. Place the wings in the bottom of the slow cooker, then pour the vinegar sauce on top. 3. Cover and cook on low for 7 to 8 hours. 4. Baste the turkey wings with the sauce from the slow cooker and serve.

Healthy Mississippi Chicken Thighs

Prep Time: 10 minutes | Cook Time: 6-8 hours | Serves: 6

3 pounds boneless, skinless chicken thighs
2 tablespoons Homemade Dry Onion Soup Mix
2 tablespoons Homemade Ranch Seasoning

8 whole pepperoncini peppers
4 tablespoons unsalted butter, cut into small pieces

1. Place the chicken thighs into the bottom of a slow cooker. 2. Sprinkle the dry onion mix and the ranch seasoning on top. 3. Add the pepperoncini, and scatter the butter pieces over the top. 4. Cook on low for 6 to 8 hours or on high for 3 to 4 hours. 5. Remove the chicken from the slow cooker and shred using two forks. Place the chicken back into the slow cooker and mix well.

Low-Carb BBQ Chicken and Onions

Prep Time: 10 minutes | Cook Time: 6-8 hours | Serves: 10

1 (3-pound) whole chicken
2 teaspoons extra-virgin olive oil
½ teaspoon salt

½ teaspoon freshly ground black pepper
1 large onion, sliced
2 cups BBQ Sauce

1. Rub the chicken all over with the olive oil and season with the salt and pepper. 2. Place the onion slices into the bottom of a slow cooker. Place the chicken on top of the onion and pour the BBQ sauce all over the chicken. 3. Cook on low for 6 to 8 hours or on high for 3 to 4 hours.

Cheese Turkey-Stuffed Peppers

Prep Time: 15 minutes | Cook Time: 7 to 8 hours | Serves: 6

1-pound lean ground turkey
1 tablespoon extra-virgin olive oil
2 teaspoons minced garlic
1 medium white onion, diced
1½ cups cooked rice
1½ teaspoons sea salt
¼ teaspoon ground black pepper
1 tablespoon dried basil

1 tablespoon dried parsley
6 yellow, orange, or red bell peppers, tops cut off and reserved, cored
¼ cup water
1 (24-ounce) jar marinara sauce
2 cups shredded mozzarella cheese
Grated Parmesan cheese, for topping
Fresh parsley, for topping

1. Combine the turkey, olive oil, onion, garlic, rice, salt, basil, black pepper, and dried parsley in a large bowl. Stir to mix well. 2. Stuff each bell pepper evenly with turkey mixture, then cover each bell pepper with its top. 3. Pour water into the slow cooker, then arrange each bell pepper inside. Cover and cook on low for 7 hours. 4. Then pour the marinara sauce over the peppers and spread the mozzarella cheese evenly on top. Cover and cook for 30 to 45 minutes longer, until the cheese has melted. 5. Once done cooking, spread the Parmesan cheese and fresh parsley on top. Serve warm. 6. Refrigerate leftovers for up to 5 days, or freeze for up to 1 month.

Lemony Chicken & Broccoli

Prep Time: 15 minutes | Cook Time: 8 hours | Serves: 10

6 teaspoons grated lemon zest, divided
1½ tablespoons Dijon mustard
1 to 2 tablespoons extra-virgin olive oil
2 teaspoons dried oregano
¼ teaspoon salt
½ teaspoon dried thyme

2 pounds bone-in, skin-on chicken thighs
⅓ cup freshly squeezed lemon juice (2 or 3 lemons)
1½ cups homemade or store-bought chicken broth
1 tablespoon butter
2 tablespoons whole-wheat flour or all-purpose gluten-free flour
1 to 2 cups fresh broccoli

1. To prepare the rub, combine 2 teaspoons of lemon zest, olive oil, oregano, mustard, salt, and thyme in a small bowl. Then cover the chicken with the rub. 2. Combine the remaining 4 teaspoons of lemon zest, lemon juice, butter, broth, and flour in your slow cooker. Whisk for 2 minutes. 3. Stir in the chicken. Cover and cook on low heat for 8 hours or until the chicken is cooked through and the lemon sauce is thickened. 4. Then add the broccoli. Cover and cook for 10 to 15 minutes more, until the broccoli is tender. 5. Serve the chicken and broccoli warm. Refrigerate leftovers.

Yogurt Chicken Stew

Prep Time: 20 minutes | Cook Time: 7 to 9 hours | Serves: 8

½ cup plain Greek yogurt
⅓ cup lemon juice
5 teaspoons curry powder
2 tablespoons grated fresh ginger root
10 (4-ounce) boneless, skinless chicken thighs

4 large tomatoes, seeded and chopped
2 onions, chopped
8 garlic cloves, sliced
⅔ cup canned coconut milk
3 tablespoons cornstarch

1. Combine the yogurt, curry powder, lemon juice, and ginger root in a medium bowl. Add the chicken and toss to coat; let rest for 15 minutes. 2. Combine the onions, tomatoes, and garlic in your slow cooker. 3. Add the chicken mixture to the slow cooker. Cover and cook on low for 7 to 9 hours, or until the chicken's internal temperature registers 165°F on a food thermometer. 4. In a small bowl, whisk together the coconut milk and cornstarch. Pour into the slow cooker and stir to mix well. 5. Cover and cook on low for 15 to 20 minutes longer, or until the sauce has thickened.

Classic Chicken Provencal

Prep Time: 20 minutes | Cook Time: 7 to 9 hours | Serves: 8

3 pounds boneless, skinless chicken thighs
3 bulbs fennel, cored and sliced
2 red bell peppers, stemmed, seeded, and chopped
2 onions, chopped
6 garlic cloves, minced

4 large tomatoes, seeded and chopped
4 sprigs fresh thyme
1 bay leaf
¼ cup sliced black Greek olives
2 tablespoons lemon juice

1. Combine all of the ingredients in the slow cooker. Cover and cook on low for 7 to 9 hours, until the internal temperature of the chicken registers 165°F on a food thermometer. 2. Remove and discard the thyme stems and bay leaf. Serve warm.

Delicious Chicken Cacciatore

Prep Time: 15 minutes | Cook Time: 6½ hours | Serves: 8

3 tablespoons water, divided
2 tablespoons whole-wheat flour
5 or 6 boneless, skinless chicken breasts
1 large white onion, diced
1 green bell pepper, cored and diced
1 red bell pepper, cored and diced
12 ounces cremini mushrooms, stemmed and chopped
1 (28-ounce) can crushed or diced tomatoes
3½ cups homemade or store-bought chicken broth

4 teaspoons minced garlic
2 tablespoons Italian seasoning
2 tablespoons red-wine vinegar
10 to 12 ounces thin spaghetti
3 (6-ounce) cans tomato paste
Sea salt
Ground black pepper
Fresh thyme leaves, for topping
1 to 1¼ cups grated Parmesan cheese, for topping

1. Grease the bottom of your slow cooker with olive oil. 2. Add 1 tablespoon of water and stir in the flour. 3. Add the chicken, onion, mushrooms, tomatoes, red bell pepper, green bell pepper, broth, garlic, vinegar, Italian seasoning, and the remaining 2 tablespoons of water. Stir to mix well. Cover and cook on low for 6 hours or until the chicken is cooked through and the vegetables are soft. 4. Then add the spaghetti and tomato paste. Stir gently. Cover and cook for 20 to 30 minutes longer, until the spaghetti is soft. 5. Spread thyme and 2 tablespoons of cheese over each serving. Season with salt and pepper to taste. Serve warm. 6. Refrigerate leftovers for up to 1 week, or freeze for up to 2 months.

Chicken and Sausage Chili

Prep Time: 10 minutes | Cook Time: 6½ to 7½ hours | Serves: 8

1½ pounds boneless, skinless chicken breasts
2½ cups thinly sliced andouille sausage
1 medium yellow onion, diced
2 teaspoons minced garlic
1½ cups homemade or store-bought chicken broth
1 (14½-ounce) can diced tomatoes, drained
¼ cup tomato paste

½ cup tomato sauce
1 tablespoon Creole seasoning
¼ cup cayenne pepper
1 tablespoon coconut sugar
1 (15-ounce) can black or kidney beans, drained and rinsed
Sliced scallions, green parts only, for topping
2 cups cooked brown or wild rice

1. Combine the chicken, sausage, garlic, onion, broth, diced tomatoes, tomato sauce, tomato paste, cayenne, Creole seasoning, and sugar in your slow cooker. Cover and cook on low for 6 to 7 hours or until the chicken and sausage are cooked through and the vegetables are soft. 2. Then transfer the chicken to a cutting board and shred it with 2 forks, then return it to the slow cooker and mix well. 3. Stir in the beans. Cover and cook for 20 to 30 minutes longer, until the beans are heated and easily mashed. 4. Once done cooking, garnish with scallions and serve warm over ¼ cup of rice per serving. 5. Refrigerate leftovers for up to 1 week, or freeze for up to 2 months.

Chicken & Carrots Casserole

Prep Time: 5 minutes | Cook Time: 8 hours | Serves: 6

1 whole chicken, separated into pieces
10 cups water
2 carrots, peeled, cut into chunks

1 onion, chopped
Seasoning: salt, pepper, thyme, rosemary to taste

1. In a nonstick skillet over medium heat, brown the onions for 5-7 minutes. 2. Add water to the slow cooker and place in the chicken separated by breast, legs, wings and thighs. 3. Add carrots, onion and seasonings to the slow cooker. 4. Cover and cook for 8 hours on low. Serve warm.

Sweet Mustard Chicken Fillets

Prep Time: 5 minutes | Cook Time: minutes | Serves: 6

6 chicken fillets, skinless, halved
¼ cup chicken broth
⅓ cup mustard, whole grain

¼ cup yacón syrup
Salt, pepper to taste

1. In a medium bowl, mix together the mustard, syrup and chicken broth. 2. Place the chicken fillets into the slow cooker. 3. Pour the mustard mixture over the chicken and season with salt and pepper. 4. Cover and cook for 6 hours on low. Serve warm.

Cheesy Chicken and Rice Casserole

Prep Time: 15 minutes | Cook Time: 6½ hours | Serves: 8

2 tablespoons extra-virgin olive oil
3 large boneless, skinless chicken breasts, chopped into bite-size pieces
2 teaspoons minced garlic
1½ teaspoons sea salt
1 teaspoon ground black pepper
1 small white onion, finely chopped

4½ cups homemade or store-bought chicken broth
2 cups sour cream or plain Greek yogurt
2¼ cups wild rice
2 cups diced carrots
2 cups shredded Cheddar, Monterey Jack, or Colby-Jack cheese
Chopped fresh parsley, for topping
1 cup grated Parmesan cheese

1. Grease the slow cooker with olive oil. 2. Add the chicken, garlic, onion, sour cream, broth, rice, carrots, salt and black pepper. Stir to mix well. Cover and cook on low for 6 hours or until the chicken is cooked through. 3. Stir in the Cheddar cheese. Cover and cook for 30 minutes longer or until the cheese is melted. 4. Spread the parsley and 2 tablespoons of Parmesan cheese over per serving. Serve warm. 5. Refrigerate leftovers for up to 5 days, or freeze for up to 2 months.

Pineapple Chicken

Prep Time: 10 minutes | Cook Time: 6 hours | Serves: 6

6 chicken thighs, boneless
8 bacon slices, 2 fried and crumbled for garnish
½ cup red onion, cut in chunks

1 cup fresh pineapple, sliced
Salt, pepper to taste

1. In a skillet over medium heat, fry 3 bacon slices until crisp. 2. Season the chicken with salt and pepper and place into the slow cooker. Spread the uncooked bacon on top. 3. Then top with onions and pineapple. 4. Cover and cook for 6 hours on low. 5. Serve with fried crisp bacon.

Homemade Bourbon Chicken

Prep Time: 15 minutes | Cook Time: 6-7 hours | Serves: 2

3 lb boneless, skinless chicken thighs
3 tbsps cornstarch
Sauce:
½ tsp fresh grated ginger
4 cloves garlic, minced
½ tsp crushed red chili flakes
⅓ cup apple juice
1½ tbsps honey
¼ cup brown sugar

¼ cup sliced green onions (or more to taste)

¼ cup ketchup
3 tbsps cider vinegar
¼ cup water
¼ cup Bourbon
¼ cup soy sauce
Salt and pepper to taste

1. In a bowl, mix together all sauce ingredients. 2. Place chicken in your slow cooker and pour the sauce over the top. Cover and cook for 6-7 hours on low or 3 hours on high. 3. Remove the chicken and cut into small pieces, set aside. 4. Mix together the water with cornstarch. Turn the heat to high and whisk the cornstarch mixture into the slow cooker. Cover and allow to thicken. Return the chicken back into the sauce and add the green onions. 5. Serve warm over rice.

Pulled Chicken Jalapeño Sandwiches

Prep Time: 10 minutes | Cook Time: 8 hours | Serves: 8

Nonstick cooking spray
2 pounds boneless, skinless chicken thighs
1 cup sliced onion
¼ cup chopped jalapeño (or hot chili) peppers

1 can (15 oz) Manwich Original Sloppy Joe Sauce
¼ tsp salt
8 Kaiser rolls

1. Spray the inside of the slow cooker with cooking spray. Add in the chicken, jalapeño, onion and Sloppy Joe sauce. Cover and cook on low for 8 hours until the chicken is tender. 2. Transfer the chicken to a serving plate and shred it. Return the chicken to the slow cooker. 3. Season with salt and serve on the rolls.

Cheese Chicken Meatballs

Prep Time: 15 minutes | Cook Time: 7 to 8 hours | Serves: 8

2 pounds ground chicken or turkey
2 large eggs
½ cup Italian-style bread crumbs
¼ cup grated Parmigiano-Reggiano cheese, plus more for serving
1 small sweet onion, finely chopped
2 tablespoons Italian seasoning

¼ teaspoon kosher salt
½ teaspoon garlic pepper or ground black pepper
5 cups marinara sauce with red lentils or store-bought low-sugar, low-sodium marinara sauce, divided
1½ cups shredded part-skim mozzarella cheese
Chopped fresh parsley, for serving

1. In a large bowl, combine the chicken, eggs, bread crumbs, onion, Italian seasoning, Parmigiano-Reggiano, salt, and garlic pepper. Using your hands, form the chicken mixture into 48 to 50 meatballs. 2. Pour 2 cups of marinara sauce into the slow cooker. Add the meatballs and cover with the remaining 3 cups of marinara sauce. 3. Cover and cook for 7 to 8 hours on low or until the meatballs are cooked through. 4. Sprinkle an even layer of mozzarella cheese over the sauce, cover and cook for 10 to 15 minutes more, until the cheese has melted. 5. Garnish with parsley and serve with additional Parmigiano-Reggiano. 6. Refrigerate leftovers for up to 4 days or freeze for up to 4 months.

Lime Salsa Chicken with Avocado

Prep Time: 10 minutes | Cook Time: 3 to 4 hours | Serves: 6

2 cups low-sodium fresh tomato salsa, divided
2 pounds boneless, skinless chicken breasts, cut into 6 pieces
1 jalapeño pepper, seeded and sliced

1 avocado, diced just before serving
1 lime, cut into 8 wedges

1. Pour 1 cup of salsa into your slow cooker. Add the chicken to the salsa in one layer, then pour in the remaining 1 cup of salsa and top with the jalapeño slices. 2. Cover and cook on low for 3 to 4 hours or until the chicken is no longer pink inside. 3. Serve with salsa, avocado, and lime wedges for squeezing on top. 4. Refrigerate leftovers for up to 4 days or freeze for up to 4 months.

Chicken, Potato & Green Bean Casserole

Prep Time: 15 minutes | Cook Time: 5 to 7 hours | Serves: 4

For the Chicken:
2 pounds boneless, skinless chicken thighs, cut into bite-size pieces
2 pounds red potatoes, cut in half
½ red onion, sliced
For the Sauce:
⅓ cup water
⅓ cup freshly squeezed lemon juice
¼ cup red wine vinegar
2 teaspoons extra-virgin olive oil

1 pound green beans, trimmed
1 cup cherry tomatoes
¼ cup pitted Kalamata olives

3 garlic cloves, minced
2 teaspoons dried oregano
½ teaspoon salt
¼ teaspoon freshly ground black pepper

1. Add the chicken, green beans, potatoes, onion, tomatoes, and olives to the slow cooker. Stir to mix well. 2. Whisk together all the sauce ingredients in a medium bowl. Pour the sauce into the slow cooker and toss until well coated. 3. Cover and cook on low for 5 to 7 hours. Serve warm.

Sweet & Spicy Chicken with Potatoes

Prep Time: 15 minutes | Cook Time: 5 to 7 hours | Serves: 4

For the Chicken:
2 pounds boneless, skinless chicken thighs
1 pound red potatoes, quartered
For the Sauce:
¾ cup honey
½ cup sriracha
¼ cup low-sodium soy sauce, tamari, or coconut aminos

2 red or green bell peppers, seeded and chopped
1 onion, chopped

2 garlic cloves, minced
2 teaspoons dried basil

1. Combine the chicken thighs, bell peppers, potatoes, and onion in the slow cooker. 2. Whisk together all the sauce ingredients in a medium bowl. Pour the sauce into the slow cooker and stir until they are well coated. 3. Cover and cook on low for 5 to 7 hours. Serve warm.

Latin Chicken & Black Beans

Prep Time: 15 minutes | Cook Time: 5 to 7 hours | Serves: 4

1 cup salsa
1 (15-ounce) can black beans, rinsed and drained
2 red or green bell peppers, seeded and sliced
1 onion, sliced
2 pounds boneless, skinless chicken thighs, cut into bite-size pieces

1 or 2 jalapeños, minced
1 garlic clove, minced
¼ cup chopped fresh cilantro
2 teaspoons ground cumin
1 teaspoon paprika

1. In your slow cooker, combine the black beans, bell peppers, salsa, and onion. Stir to mix well. 2. Then stir in the chicken, cilantro, jalapeños, cumin, and paprika, and toss to combine. 3. Cover and cook on low for 5 to 7 hours. Serve warm.

Curried Chicken Stew

Prep Time: 15 minutes | Cook Time: 5 to 7 hours | Serves: 4

2 pounds boneless, skinless chicken thighs
1 (15-ounce) can coconut cream or full-fat coconut milk
1 onion, diced
1 (6-ounce) can tomato paste
1½ teaspoons ghee
3 tablespoons freshly squeezed lime juice
3 garlic cloves, minced

2 teaspoons ground cumin
1 teaspoon ground ginger
1 teaspoon ground coriander
1 teaspoon curry powder
1 teaspoon salt
¼ cup chopped fresh cilantro, for garnish

1. In the slow cooker, combine all the ingredients except the cilantro and stir to mix well. 2. Cover and cook on low heat for 5 to 7 hours. 3. Garnish with the fresh cilantro before serving.

Turkey Breast with Gravy

Prep Time: 10 minutes | Cook Time: 8 hours | Serves: 8

1 tablespoon olive oil
2 teaspoons garlic powder
½ teaspoon dried crushed rosemary
½ teaspoon dried thyme
½ teaspoon ground sage
½ teaspoon onion powder

½ teaspoon salt, plus more for seasoning
½ teaspoon freshly ground black pepper, plus more for seasoning
1 (4-pound) bone-in turkey breast
2 tablespoons cornstarch
2 tablespoons water

1. In a small bowl, mix together the olive oil, garlic powder, thyme, sage, rosemary, onion powder, salt, and pepper. Rub the herb mixture all over the turkey breast. Then place the turkey in the slow cooker. 2. Cover and cook on low heat for 8 hours, or until the internal temperature at the thickest part of the breast registers 165°F. 3. Transfer the cooked turkey to a cutting board. Tent with aluminum foil and let it rest for 10 minutes. 4. Meanwhile, you can prepare the gravy. Carefully pour the drippings from the slow cooker through a fine-mesh strainer into a saucepan over medium-high heat. Whisk together the cornstarch and water in a small bowl. Add the cornstarch slurry to the saucepan with the drippings. Stir frequently until the mixture bubbles and thickens, about 5 minutes. 5. Season with more salt and pepper, if needed. 6. Slice the turkey and serve with the gravy.

Cheese Chicken Lettuce Wraps

Prep Time: 10 minutes | Cook Time: 6 to 7 hours | Serves: 8

2 tablespoons buttermilk powder
1 teaspoon garlic pepper
1 teaspoon onion powder
2 teaspoons dried parsley
¾ teaspoon dried dill
¼ teaspoon kosher salt
3 pounds boneless, skinless chicken breasts

1 (8-ounce) package reduced-fat cream cheese, cubed
1 cup shredded Monterey Jack cheese
Large lettuce leaves (preferably Bibb), for serving
6 turkey bacon slices, cooked and crumbled, for serving
Chopped scallions, green and white parts, for serving
Chopped fresh chives, for serving
Hot sauce, for serving (optional)

1. Whisk together the buttermilk powder, onion powder, garlic pepper, dill, parsley, and salt in a small bowl. 2. Place the chicken in a single layer in the slow cooker. Sprinkle with the seasoning mix and top with the cream cheese. 3. Cover and cook on low for 6 to 7 hours or until the chicken is no longer pink. 4. Then shred the chicken in the slow cooker with 2 forks and mix it with the softened cream cheese. Spread the Monterey Jack cheese on top. Cover and let sit for 10 to 15 minutes until the cheese melts. 5. Once done, spoon some of the chicken mixture into lettuce leaves. Top with the bacon, scallions, chives, and hot sauce (if using). Serve immediately. 6. Refrigerate leftovers for up to 4 days. This dish does not freeze well.

Herb-Garlic Turkey Legs

Prep Time: 10 minutes | Cook Time: 5 to 7 hours | Serves: 4

2 tablespoons extra-virgin olive oil
4 medium turkey legs (about 3 pounds total)
1 tablespoon paprika
1 tablespoon garlic powder

1 tablespoon oregano
2 teaspoons salt
2 teaspoons freshly ground black pepper

1. Rub the turkey legs evenly with oil. 2. In a small bowl, mix the seasonings together and rub them on each turkey leg. 3. Put the turkey legs in the slow cooker. 4. Cover and cook on low for 5 to 7 hours. Serve warm.

Shredded Chicken Tacos

Prep Time: 10 minutes | Cook Time: 6 hours | Serves: 6

2 pounds boneless, skinless chicken thighs, trimmed of excess fat
Salt
Freshly ground black pepper
1 (10-ounce) can diced tomatoes with green chiles
1 teaspoon ground cumin

1 teaspoon garlic powder
Corn taco shells or soft flour tortillas
Optional toppings: shredded cheese, sour cream, guacamole, fresh lime juice, chopped fresh cilantro, shredded lettuce, diced tomatoes

1. Place the chicken in the slow cooker and season with salt and pepper. Add the tomatoes with their juice, garlic powder and cumin to the slow cooker. Stir to combine. 2. Cover and cook on low for 6 hours, until the chicken is tender. 3. Transfer the chicken to a cutting board and shred them with two forks. Return the chicken to the slow cooker and stir to mix well. Season with more salt and pepper, if needed. 4. Serve the chicken in taco shells or tortillas with your favorite toppings.

Tomatillo Chicken Stew

Prep Time: 15 minutes | Cook Time: 6 hours | Serves: 6

2 pounds boneless, skinless chicken thighs, trimmed of excess fat
2½ teaspoons ground cumin, divided
2 teaspoons dried oregano
1½ teaspoons garlic powder
1¾ teaspoons salt, divided

½ teaspoon freshly ground black pepper
8 tomatillos, husked and halved
1 red onion, cut into wedges
1 poblano chile, cut into quarters and seeded
2 teaspoons fresh lime juice

1. Place the chicken in the slow cooker and sprinkle with 2 teaspoons of cumin, garlic powder, oregano, 1 teaspoon of salt, and black pepper. Nestle the tomatillo halves, onion and poblano around the chicken. 2. Cover and cook on low heat for 6 hours, or until the chicken is tender. 3. Transfer the chicken to a cutting board and use 2 forks to shred the chicken. 4. Carefully pour the mixture in the slow cooker through a fine-mesh strainer into a bowl. Transfer the solids from the strainer to a food processor and pulse until semi-smooth. Reserve the liquid in the bowl. 5. Return the chicken and sauce in the blender to the slow cooker. Sprinkle with the remaining salt and cumin, and add the lime juice. 6. If you prefer a thinner sauce, stir in some of the reserved liquid. Serve.

Herbed Delicious Orange Chicken Thighs

Prep Time: 20 minutes | Cook Time: 7 to 9 hours | Serves: 8

10 (4-ounce) boneless, skinless chicken thighs
2 tablespoons honey
3 tablespoons grated fresh ginger root
1 teaspoon ground red chili
1 tablespoon chili powder

½ teaspoon ground cloves
¼ teaspoon ground allspice
3 onions, chopped
6 garlic cloves, minced
½ cup freshly squeezed orange juice

1. Cut slashes across the chicken thighs. 2. Mix together the honey, ginger root, chili powder, cloves, ground chili, and allspice in a small bowl. Rub the chicken with this mixture. Set aside. 3. Place the onions and garlic in the bottom of the slow cooker. Spread the chicken on top and pour the orange juice over all. 4. Cover the lid and cook on low for 7 to 9 hours, or until a food thermometer registers 165°F. Serve warm.

Chapter 4 Beef, Pork and Lamb

Flavorful Italian Pork with Beans and Greens

Prep Time: 10 minutes | Cook Time: 8-9 hours | Serves: 8

Nonstick cooking spray
2 pounds pork shoulder, visible fat removed
1 teaspoon dried basil
1 teaspoon dried oregano
1 onion, chopped
2 medium carrots, sliced

4 garlic cloves, minced
1 cup low-sodium chicken broth
1 (14.5-ounce) can no-salt-added diced tomatoes
1 (15-ounce) can cannellini beans, drained and rinsed
2 cups chopped fresh green beans
2 cups chopped spinach

1. Spray the inside of a 6-quart slow cooker with the cooking spray. Add the pork and sprinkle it with the basil and oregano. Add the onion, carrots, and garlic and pour in the stock and tomatoes. Cover and cook on low for 7 to 8 hours. 2. Break up the meat into large chunks. Add the cannellini beans, green beans, and spinach. Cover and continue cooking for 1 hour more, until the vegetables are tender and the internal temperature of the pork reaches 160°F.
3. Serve hot, with the potatoes or rice if desired.

Easy All-In-One Lamb-Vegetable Dinner

Prep Time: 10 minutes | Cook Time: 6 hours | Serves: 4

¼ cup extra-virgin olive oil, divided
1 pound boneless lamb chops, about ½-inch thick
Salt, for seasoning
Freshly ground black pepper, for seasoning
½ sweet onion, sliced

½ fennel bulb, cut into 2-inch chunks
1 zucchini, cut into 1-inch chunks
¼ cup chicken broth
2 tablespoons chopped fresh basil, for garnish

1. Lightly grease the insert of the slow cooker with 1 tablespoon of the olive oil. 2. Season the lamb with salt and pepper. 3. In a medium bowl, toss together the onion, fennel, and zucchini with the remaining 3 tablespoons of the olive oil and then place half of the vegetables in the insert. 4. Place the lamb on top of the vegetables, cover with the remaining vegetables, and add the broth. 5. Cover and cook on low for 6 hours. 6. Serve topped with the basil.

Rosemary Lamb Shanks with Wild Mushroom

Prep Time: 15 minutes | Cook Time: 7-8 hours | Serves: 6

3 tablespoons extra-virgin olive oil, divided
2 pounds lamb shanks
½ pound wild mushrooms, sliced
1 leek, thoroughly cleaned and chopped
2 celery stalks, chopped
1 carrot, diced

1 tablespoon minced garlic
1 (15-ounce) can crushed tomatoes
½ cup beef broth
2 tablespoons apple cider vinegar
1 teaspoon dried rosemary
½ cup sour cream, for garnish

1. Lightly grease the insert of the slow cooker with 1 tablespoon of the olive oil. 2. In a large skillet over medium-high heat, heat the remaining 2 tablespoons of the olive oil. add the lamb; brown for 6 minutes, turning once; and transfer to the insert. 3. In the skillet, sauté the mushrooms, leek, celery, carrot, and garlic for 5 minutes. 4. Transfer the vegetables to the insert along with the tomatoes, broth, apple cider vinegar, and rosemary. 5. Cover and cook on low for 7 to 8 hours. 6. Serve topped with the sour cream.

Coconut Curried Lamb

Prep Time: 15 minutes | Cook Time: 7-8 hours | Serves: 6

3 tablespoons extra-virgin olive oil, divided
1½ pounds lamb shoulder chops
Salt, for seasoning
Freshly ground black pepper, for seasoning
3 cups coconut milk
½ sweet onion, sliced

¼ cup curry powder
1 tablespoon grated fresh ginger
2 teaspoons minced garlic
1 carrot, diced
2 tablespoons chopped cilantro, for garnish

1. Lightly grease the insert of the slow cooker with 1 tablespoon of the olive oil. 2. In a large skillet over medium-high heat, heat the remaining 2 tablespoons of the olive oil. 3. Season the lamb with the salt and pepper. Add the lamb to the skillet and brown for 6 minutes, turning once. Transfer to the insert. 4. Stir together the coconut milk, onion, curry, ginger, and garlic in a medium bowl. 5. Add the mixture to the lamb along with the carrot. 6. Cover and cook on low for 7 to 8 hours. 7. Serve topped with the cilantro.

Rosemary Lamb Chops with Onions

Prep Time: 15 minutes | Cook Time: 6 hours | Serves: 4

3 tablespoons extra-virgin olive oil, divided
1½ pounds lamb shoulder chops
Salt, for seasoning
Freshly ground black pepper, for seasoning
½ cup chicken broth

1 sweet onion, sliced
2 teaspoons minced garlic
2 teaspoons dried rosemary
1 teaspoon dried thyme

1. Lightly grease the insert of the slow cooker with 1 tablespoon of the olive oil. 2. In a large skillet over medium-high heat, heat the remaining 2 tablespoons of the olive oil. 3. Season the lamb with the salt and pepper. Add the lamb to the skillet and brown for 6 minutes, turning once. 4. Transfer the lamb to the insert, and add the broth, onion, garlic, rosemary, and thyme. 5. Cover and cook on low for 6 hours. 6. Serve warm.

Spicy Tender Lamb Roast

Prep Time: 10 minutes | Cook Time: 7-8 hours | Serves: 6

1 tablespoon extra-virgin olive oil
2 pounds lamb shoulder roast
salt, for seasoning
Freshly ground black pepper, for seasoning
1 (14.5-ounce) can diced tomatoes
1 tablespoon cumin

2 teaspoons minced garlic
1 teaspoon paprika
1 teaspoon chili powder
1 cup sour cream
2 teaspoons chopped fresh parsley, for garnish

1. Lightly grease the insert of the slow cooker with the olive oil. 2. Lightly season the lamb with the salt and pepper. 3. Place the lamb in the insert and add the tomatoes, cumin, garlic, paprika, and chili powder. 4. Cover and cook on low for 7 to 8 hours. 5. Stir in the sour cream. 6. Serve topped with the parsley.

Tunisian Lamb Ragout with Pumpkin and Carrots

Prep Time: 15 minutes | Cook Time: 8 hours | Serves: 6

¼ cup extra-virgin olive oil
1½ pounds lamb shoulder, cut into 1-inch chunks
1 sweet onion, chopped
1 tablespoon minced garlic
4 cups pumpkin, cut into 1-inch pieces
2 carrots, diced

1 (14.5-ounce) can diced tomatoes
3 cups beef broth
2 tablespoons ras el hanout
1 teaspoon hot chili powder
1 teaspoon salt
1 cup greek yogurt

1. Lightly grease the slow cooker insert with 1 tablespoon olive oil. 2. In a large skillet over medium–high heat, add the remaining oil. 3. Brown the lamb for 6 minutes, then add the onion and garlic. 4. Sauté for 3 minutes more, then transfer the lamb and vegetables to the insert. 5. Add the pumpkin, carrots, tomatoes, broth, ras el hanout, chili powder, and salt to the insert and stir to combine. 6. Cover and cook on low for 8 hours. 7. Serve topped with the yogurt.

Cheesy Steak Roulades with Spinach & Olives

Prep Time: 15 minutes | Cook Time: 6 hours | Serves: 4

4 (5-ounce) pieces skirt steak, pounded to ½-inch thickness
½ teaspoon kosher salt
½ teaspoon freshly ground black pepper
4 cups chopped baby spinach
1 small onion, diced
1 cup grated Parmesan cheese

4 ounces feta cheese, crumbled
½ cup chopped Kalamata olives
¼ cup beef broth or water
5 tablespoons unsalted butter or ghee
1 cup heavy (whipping) cream

1. Season the steak all over with the salt and pepper. 2. In a medium bowl, mix the onion, Parmesan, spinach, feta, and olives. Top each steak with one-quarter of the mixture, placing it close to one of the short sides. Starting with the short side closest to the filling, roll the steaks around the filling. Use wooden toothpicks or kitchen twine, if needed, to secure the rolls. Arrange the rolls in a single layer in the slow cooker. 3. Pour in the beef broth. Cover and cook for 6 hours on low or 3 hours on high. When finished, remove the roulades from the slow cooker and let them rest for a few minutes. 4. While the roulades are resting, place the butter and heavy cream into the slow cooker and stir to melt the butter and mix well with the cooking juices. 5. Slice the roulades into pinwheels and serve hot, with the cream sauce spooned over the top.

Chili Sesame Short Ribs Braised in Coconut Milk

Prep Time: 10 minutes | Cook Time: 9 hours | Serves: 6

1 onion, diced
3 garlic cloves, minced
1 tablespoon minced fresh ginger
1 (14-ounce) can coconut milk
2 tablespoons soy sauce, tamari, or coconut aminos
2 tablespoons mirin
2 tablespoons toasted sesame oil

2 teaspoons blackstrap molasses
1 teaspoon or less chili paste for seasoning
1 teaspoon stevia powder
1 pound short ribs
3 scallions, thinly sliced
¼ cup toasted sesame seeds

1. Stir together the sesame oil, onion, garlic, ginger, coconut milk, soy sauce, mirin, molasses, chili paste, and stevia powder in the slow cooker. 2. Add the short ribs and stir to coat them well. Cover and cook for 9 hours on low or 4½ hours on high. 3. When finished, serve hot, garnished with the scallions and sesame seeds.

North African Braised Beef with Almonds

Prep Time: 10 minutes | Cook Time: 9 hours | Serves: 4-6

¼ cup coconut oil
1 medium onion, diced
2 teaspoons ground cumin
1½ teaspoons kosher salt
½ teaspoon freshly ground black pepper
½ teaspoon ground cinnamon
½ teaspoon ground ginger

1 cup dry red wine
1 (1¼-pound) beef chuck roast, cut into 2-inch pieces
Grated zest and juice of 1 orange
1 cup heavy (whipping) cream
5 tablespoons unsalted butter
½ cup ground toasted almonds
¼ cup chopped fresh cilantro

1. In a large skillet, heat the coconut oil over medium-high heat. Add the onion and sauté until soft, about 5 minutes. 2. Add the cumin, salt, cinnamon, pepper, and ginger. Sauté for 1 minute more. 3. Stir in the red wine and bring to a boil. Cook for 1 to 2 minutes and scrape up any browned bits from the bottom of the pan. Transfer the mixture to the slow cooker. 4. Stir in the beef, orange zest, and orange juice. Cover and cook for 9 hours on low or 4½ hours on high. 5. Place in the heavy cream and butter to stir until the butter melts and both are well incorporated.

Classic Greek Lamb & Eggplant Casserole

Prep Time: 15 minutes | Cook Time: 8 hours | Serves: 6

1 large eggplant, peeled and cut into ¼-inch-thick slices
1¼ pounds ground lamb
1 (14.5-ounce) can diced tomatoes, drained
1 cup tomato sauce
1 onion, diced
5 garlic cloves, minced
1 teaspoon dried oregano
1 teaspoon kosher salt

1 teaspoon freshly ground black pepper
½ teaspoon ground nutmeg
½ teaspoon ground cinnamon
1 cup heavy (whipping) cream
3 large egg yolks
¾ cup feta cheese
2 tablespoons minced fresh parsley

1. In the bottom of the slow cooker, arrange half of the eggplant slices. They should cover the bottom completely, overlapping as necessary. 2. In a large skillet, sauté the lamb over medium-high heat until browned, about 5 minutes. Using a slotted spoon, transfer the meat to a large bowl, leaving any excess fat behind in the skillet. 3. Add the tomatoes, tomato sauce, onion, garlic, oregano, salt, nutmeg, pepper, and cinnamon to the lamb. Stir to mix well. Spread the meat mixture over the eggplant slices in the slow cooker and arrange the remaining eggplant slices over the top. 4. In a medium bowl, whisk together the heavy cream, egg yolks, and feta cheese. Pour this over the ingredients in the slow cooker. Cover and cook for 8 hours on low. 5. When finished, serve hot, garnished with the parsley.

Garlic Barbecue Meatballs

Prep Time: 5 minutes | Cook Time: 1 hour | Serves: 12

1 (18-ounce) bottle barbecue sauce
2 teaspoons onion powder
1 teaspoon garlic powder

1 (32-ounce) package pre-cooked meatballs (beef or chicken), such as of Tov

1. In a medium-sized mixing bowl, combine barbecue sauce, onion powder, and garlic powder. 2. Pour about 1 cup of sauce into a 4-quart slow cooker. Add the meatballs. 3. Pour remaining barbecue sauce over meatballs. Cover and cook on high for 1 hour. 4. When finished, serve.

Coconut Lamb Curry

Prep Time: 10 minutes | Cook Time: 8 hours | Serves: 6

1½ pounds lamb stew meat, cut into 1½-inch cubes
1 onion, diced
2 garlic cloves, minced
1 tablespoon grated fresh ginger
1 tablespoon curry powder
1 teaspoon kosher salt

¾ teaspoon freshly ground black pepper
½ teaspoon cayenne pepper
1 (14-ounce) can coconut milk
¼ cup coconut oil, melted
½ cup ground toasted almonds (optional)
8 to 10 whole curry leaves or ½ cup chopped fresh cilantro

1. In the slow cooker, combine the lamb, onion, garlic, black pepper, ginger, curry powder, salt, and cayenne pepper. 2. Place in the coconut milk and coconut oil and stir to mix. Cover and cook for 8 hours on low or 4 hours on high. 3. When finished, serve hot, garnished with the ground almonds (if using) and curry leaves.

Braised Tender Lamb with Fennel

Prep Time: 15 minutes | Cook Time: 8 hours | Serves: 4

1½ pounds lamb stew meat, cut into 2-inch pieces
1 teaspoon kosher salt
½ teaspoon freshly ground black pepper
¼ cup (½ stick) unsalted butter, ghee, or coconut oil
1 onion, sliced
1 cup sliced fennel
1 (14.5-ounce) can diced tomatoes, drained
½ cup dry red wine

2 tablespoons tomato paste
2 garlic cloves, minced
2 teaspoons paprika
Pinch stevia powder
1 cinnamon stick
1 cup heavy (whipping) cream
¾ cup chopped pistachios
2 tablespoons chopped fresh mint

1. Season the lamb with the salt and pepper. 2. In a large skillet, heat the butter over medium-high heat. Place the lamb and cook until browned on all sides, about 8 minutes. Transfer the meat to the slow cooker. 3. Return the skillet to medium-high heat and add the onion and fennel. Sauté until softened, about 3 minutes. 4. Stir in the tomatoes, red wine, tomato paste, garlic, paprika, stevia, and cinnamon. Bring to a boil. Transfer the sauce to the cooker. Cover and cook for 8 hours on low. 5. Just before serving, discard the cinnamon stick and stir in the heavy cream. Serve hot, garnished with the pistachios and mint.

Yummy Creamy Swedish Meatballs

Prep Time: 15 minutes | Cook Time: 2-4 hours 15 minutes | Serves: 20

Cooking spray
Meatballs:
2 thin slices white sandwich bread, torn into ½ inch pieces
½ cup soymilk
2 pounds lean ground beef
2 cloves garlic, minced
Sauce:
1 tablespoon olive oil
⅓ cup all-purpose flour
3 cups low-sodium chicken broth
1½ cups pareve nondairy creamer such as Rich's

1 egg
¼ teaspoon salt
¼ teaspoon allspice
⅛ teaspoon nutmeg

¼ teaspoon allspice
⅛ teaspoon nutmeg
¼ teaspoon salt
¼ teaspoon white pepper

1. Preheat the oven to 400°F. Line 2 rimmed baking sheets with foil and spray each lightly with nonstick spray. 2. To make the meatballs, place the bread pieces into a large bowl. Pour in the soymilk and let the bread soak for a minute. Add the meat, garlic, egg, salt, allspice, and nutmeg. Using clean hands, mix it all together just until combined. 3. Form the mixture into 1" balls and divide balls evenly between the baking sheets. Bake the meatballs until they just begin to color, 10–15 minutes. Drain the meatballs on paper towel–lined plates, then transfer to the slow cooker. 4. To make the sauce, while the meatballs are cooking, warm the oil over medium heat in a 3-quart saucepan. When melted, place in the flour and stir to combine. Slowly stream in the chicken broth, whisking constantly to avoid lumps. Whisk in the pareve nondairy creamer, allspice, nutmeg, salt, and pepper. Simmer until the mixture thickens slightly, then remove from heat. 5. Pour sauce over meatballs. Cover and cook on low for 2–4 hours. 6. When finished, serve.

Hoisin Mongolian Beef

Prep Time: 5 minutes | Cook Time: 5 hours 20 minutes | Serves: 6

3 pounds lean beef roast, extra fat removed
3 cloves garlic, grated
1 knob peeled fresh ginger, grated, or 1 teaspoon ground ginger
1 medium onion, thinly sliced
½ cup water
½ cup low-sodium soy sauce

2 tablespoons balsamic vinegar
2 tablespoons hoisin sauce
1 tablespoon five-spice powder
1 tablespoon cornstarch
1 teaspoon red pepper flakes
1 teaspoon sesame oil

1. Place all ingredients in a 4-quart slow cooker. Cover and cook for 5 hours on low or until the thoroughly cooked through and tender. 2. Remove the roast to a cutting board. Slice thinly and return it to the slow cooker. Cook for another 20 minutes on high. Stir the meat and the sauce before serving.

Traditional Cincinnati Chili

Prep Time: 10 minutes | Cook Time: 5 hours | Serves: 4

1 tablespoon vegetable oil
1 onion, chopped
3 cloves garlic, minced
1 pound ground beef
1 cup tomato sauce
1 cup water
2 tablespoons red wine vinegar
2 tablespoons chili powder

½ teaspoon cumin
½ teaspoon ground cinnamon
½ teaspoon sweet paprika
½ teaspoon ground cinnamon
1 tablespoon light brown sugar
1 tablespoon unsweetened cocoa powder
1 teaspoon hot pepper sauce
16 ounces cooked spaghetti

1. Heat the oil in a large skillet over medium-high heat. Add onion and garlic. Sauté for about 3–4 minutes, or until onions start to soften. 2. Push everything to the sides of the pan, then add the ground beef. With a wooden spoon, break up meat, then cook, and stir occasionally, until meat is browned and no pink remains. 3. Pour off grease, then add meat to a 4-quart slow cooker. Top with all ingredients except for the spaghetti. Cover and cook on low heat for 5 hours. 4. When finished, serve the chili over the spaghetti.

Flavorful Semi-Spicy Beef Chili

Prep Time: 10 minutes | Cook Time: 4-6 hours | Serves: 4

1 tablespoon vegetable oil
1 medium onion, peeled and diced
2 cloves garlic, minced
1 chili in adobo sauce, finely diced
1 pound lean ground beef

2 (14.5-ounce) cans fire-roasted diced tomatoes
2 teaspoons chili powder
1 teaspoon ground cumin
Pinch cayenne pepper
Pareve shredded pepper jack "cheese" (optional)

1. Heat the oil in a large skillet over medium-high heat. Add onion and garlic. Sauté for about 3–4 minutes, or until onions start to soften. Stir in the chili in adobo sauce. 2. Push everything to the sides of the pan, then add the ground beef. With a wooden spoon, break up meat, then cook, and stir occasionally, until meat is browned and no pink remains. 3. Pour off grease, then add meat to a 4-quart slow cooker. Drain 1 can of tomatoes and discard liquid. Add the drained tomatoes, the remaining can of tomatoes and their liquid, chili powder, cumin, and cayenne pepper to the slow cooker. 4. Cover and cook on low for 4–6 hours. 5. When finished, divide the chili among 5 dishes and serve hot, topped with the pareve "cheese" if desired.

Delicious Chimichurri Pork and Bell Peppers

Prep Time: 5 minutes | Cook Time: 8-10 hours | Serves: 8

2½ pounds lean pork loin
2 bell peppers, seeded and chopped
1 small onion, chopped

½ teaspoon salt
¼ teaspoon freshly ground black pepper
1 cup Chimichurri Sauce

1. Add the pork, bell peppers, onion, salt, and black pepper to a slow cooker. Pour the chimichurri over the top. 2. Cook on low for 8 to 10 hours or on high for 4 to 5 hours. 3. When finished, serve.

Homemade Moroccan-Style Lamb Stew

Prep Time: 10 minutes | Cook Time: 8-10 hours | Serves: 6

Cooking spray
½ cup chicken broth
1 pinch saffron threads, lightly crushed
2 pounds lamb stew meat, cut into 1" cubes
1 medium onion, diced
¼ cup golden raisins
½ cup dried apricots, cut into halves

½ teaspoon ground ginger
1 teaspoon ground cinnamon
1 teaspoon kosher salt
¼ teaspoon black pepper
3 cups cooked couscous
4 tablespoons toasted slivered almonds (for garnish)

1. Lightly spray inside of a 6-quart slow cooker with cooking spray. 2. In a heat-safe bowl, mix the chicken broth with the crushed saffron threads. Heat the mixture for 30 seconds in a microwave at full power. 3. Place the lamb, onion, raisins, and apricots in the prepared slow cooker. Sprinkle with the remaining spices. Pour the broth mixture over spices. Cover and cook on low for 8–10 hours. 4. When finished, serve over the couscous and garnish with the almonds, if desired.

Healthy Bacon-Wrapped Meatloaf

Prep Time: 5 minutes | Cook Time: 6-8 hours | Serves: 8

1 pound bacon
1 pound 93% lean ground beef
1 cup low-sodium or no-salt-added diced tomatoes
1 small egg
1 small onion, diced

2 garlic cloves, minced
¼ cup almond flour
1 tablespoon Italian seasoning
1 teaspoon salt
½ teaspoon freshly ground black pepper

1. Weave the bacon strips into a basket weave pattern and lie flat on a cutting board. 2. In a large bowl, mix together the ground beef, tomatoes, egg, onion, garlic, almond flour, Italian seasoning, salt, and pepper. Form the mixture into a rough loaf shape and place it on top of the woven bacon strips. 3. Wrap the bacon around the meatloaf, tucking the slices into the meat to secure. Place the bacon-wrapped meatloaf into a slow cooker, seam-side down. 4. Cook on low for 6 to 8 hours or on high for 3 to 4 hours. 5. If you want your bacon crisp, finish by placing the cooked bacon-wrapped meatloaf on a rimmed baking sheet and broil in the oven for 5 to 10 minutes.

Balsamic Mustard Beef Roast

Prep Time: 5 minutes | Cook Time: 8-10 hours | Serves: 6

½ cup low-sodium beef broth
⅓ cup balsamic vinegar
1 tablespoon Dijon mustard
1 (3-pound) boneless lean chuck roast, trimmed of fat

¼ teaspoon salt
¼ teaspoon freshly ground black pepper
4 carrots, peeled and chopped
1 medium onion, chopped

1. In a small bowl, whisk together the broth, balsamic vinegar, and mustard until well blended. 2. Season the roast with the salt and pepper and place in the bottom of a slow cooker. Place the carrots and onion around the roast. 3. Pour the broth mixture over the top. 4. Cook on low for 8 to 10 hours or on high for 4 to 5 hours. 5. When finished, serve.

Authentic Beef Shawarma Roast

Prep Time: 10 minutes | Cook Time: 8-10 hours | Serves: 8

1 small onion, sliced
3 garlic cloves, minced
1 (3-pound) boneless lean beef shoulder pot roast, trimmed of fat
¼ cup Bone Broth
3 tablespoons white vinegar
3 tablespoons freshly squeezed lemon juice
2 tablespoons extra-virgin olive oil
1 tablespoon water

2 teaspoons allspice
1 teaspoon nutmeg
1 teaspoon cardamom
1 teaspoon garlic powder
½ teaspoon salt
½ teaspoon freshly ground black pepper
¼ teaspoon cinnamon
¼ cup finely chopped fresh parsley

1. Place the onion and garlic in the bottom of a slow cooker. Place the roast on top. 2. In a small bowl, mix together the broth, vinegar, lemon juice, olive oil, water, allspice, nutmeg, cardamom, garlic powder, salt, pepper, and cinnamon. Pour the sauce over the roast in the slow cooker. 3. Cook on low for 8 to 10 hours or on high for 4 to 5 hours. 4. When finished, garnish with the parsley.

Easy Philly Cheesesteak Wraps

Prep Time: 10 minutes | Cook Time: 4-6 hours 15 minutes | Serves: 6

2 pounds lean beef sirloin, sliced
2 bell peppers, seeded and sliced
1 large onion, sliced
4 ounces mushrooms, sliced
1 tablespoon Ghee
⅓ cup low-sodium beef broth
1 teaspoon steak seasoning

½ teaspoon garlic powder
¼ teaspoon freshly ground black pepper
¼ teaspoon parsley
¼ teaspoon salt (optional if your steak seasoning doesn't include it)
6 slices provolone cheese
1 head iceberg lettuce

1. Add the beef, bell peppers, onion, mushrooms, ghee, broth, steak seasoning, garlic powder, black pepper, parsley, and salt (if using) to a slow cooker. Stir to mix well. 2. Cook on low for 4 to 6 hours or on high for 2 to 3 hours. 3. Stir to mix again and layer the provolone slices across the top of the mixture. 4. Cook an additional 10 to 15 minutes on high or until the cheese is melted. Spoon onto lettuce leaves, wrap, and serve immediately.

Aromatic Jerk Pork Chops

Prep Time: 5 minutes | Cook Time: 4-6 hours | Serves: 4

4 (6-ounce) bone-in pork chops, trimmed of fat
1 small onion, sliced
2 garlic cloves, minced
⅓ cup low-sodium chicken broth
1 teaspoon extra-virgin olive oil
1 teaspoon parsley
1 teaspoon dried chopped onion
½ teaspoon garlic powder

½ teaspoon thyme
½ teaspoon salt
½ teaspoon nutmeg
½ teaspoon allspice
½ teaspoon freshly ground black pepper
¼ teaspoon red pepper flakes
¼ teaspoon cayenne pepper
¼ teaspoon cinnamon

1. Place the pork chops, onion, and garlic into a slow cooker. 2. In a small bowl, mix together the broth, olive oil, parsley, dried onion, garlic powder, thyme, salt, nutmeg, allspice, black pepper, red pepper flakes, cayenne, and cinnamon. Pour the mixture over the pork chops. 3. Cook on low for 4 to 6 hours or on high for 2 to 3 hours. 4. When finished, serve.

Lamb Meatballs with Avocado-Dill Sauce

Prep Time: 10 minutes | Cook Time: 7 to 8 hours | Serves: 12

1½ pounds ground lamb
1 small white onion, minced
1 large egg
1 teaspoon garlic powder
½ teaspoon sea salt

½ teaspoon ground cumin
½ teaspoon pumpkin pie spice
½ teaspoon paprika
¼ teaspoon freshly ground black pepper
1 cup avocado-dill sauce

1. In a large bowl, combine the lamb, onion, egg, salt, cumin, garlic powder, paprika, pumpkin pie spice, and pepper. Stir to mix well. Form the lamb mixture into 12 equal meatballs. Arrange the meatballs in the bottom of your slow cooker. 2. Cover and cook on low for 7 to 8 hours. 3. Serve with the avocado-dill sauce.

Herbed Leg of Lamb

Prep Time: 15 minutes | Cook Time: 5 to 6 hours | Serves: 6

1½ teaspoons sea salt
½ teaspoon freshly ground black pepper
1 teaspoon garlic powder
1 teaspoon dried thyme leaves
1 teaspoon dried rosemary

1 teaspoons Dijon mustard
1 (4-pound) bone-in lamb leg
2 cups broth of choice
1 small onion, roughly chopped

1. In a small bowl, mix together the salt, pepper, thyme, rosemary, garlic powder, and mustard to make a paste. Rub the lamb evenly with the paste, and place it in the slow cooker. 2. Add the broth and onion around the lamb. 3. Cover and cook on low for 5 to 6 hours and serve.

Homemade Meatloaf

Prep Time: 15 minutes | Cook Time: minutes | Serves: 4

1-pound lean ground beef
1 small onion, diced
1 cup fresh spinach, minced well
1 large egg, whisked well
½ cup unsweetened almond milk
½ cup all-natural ketchup (choose the one with the lowest amount of

sugar)
½ teaspoon sea salt
½ teaspoon garlic powder
½ teaspoon dried sage, minced
½ teaspoon Dijon mustard

1. Combine the ground beef, egg, onion, almond milk, spinach, ketchup, salt, sage, garlic powder, and mustard in your slow cooker. Stir to mix well. Form the meat mixture into a loaf shape and arrange it in the center of the slow cooker. 2. Cover and cook on low for 5 to 6 hours, or until the center of the meatloaf reaches 160°F measured with a meat thermometer. Serve.

Beef & Bell Pepper Stew

Prep Time: 15 minutes | Cook Time: 6 to 7 hours | Serves: 4

1-pound beef tenderloin, cut into 1-inch chunks
1 red bell pepper, seeded and roughly chopped
1 yellow bell pepper, seeded and roughly chopped
1 green bell pepper, seeded and roughly chopped
1 medium onion, chopped
1 (14-ounce) can diced tomatoes
1 cup beef bone broth or store-bought broth of choice

¼ cup coconut aminos
1½ teaspoons garlic powder
1 teaspoon coconut sugar
½ teaspoon ground ginger
Dash hot sauce (optional)
Freshly ground black pepper

1. Combine the beef, bell peppers, tomatoes, onion, broth, coconut aminos, ginger, garlic powder, coconut sugar, hot sauce (if using), and black pepper in your slow cooker. 2. Cover and cook on low for 6 to 7 hours and serve.

Beef Lettuce Wraps

Prep Time: 15 minutes | Cook Time: 7 to 8 hours | Serves: 6

2 pounds beef chuck roast
1 small white onion, diced
1 cup broth of choice
3 tablespoons coconut aminos
2 tablespoons coconut sugar
1 tablespoon rice vinegar
1 teaspoon garlic powder

1 teaspoon sesame oil
½ teaspoon ground ginger
¼ teaspoon red pepper flakes
8 romaine lettuce leaves
1 tablespoon sesame seeds (optional)
2 scallions (both white and green parts), diced (optional)

1. Combine the beef, onion, coconut aminos, broth, vinegar, coconut sugar, ginger, garlic powder, sesame oil, and red pepper flakes in the slow cooker. 2. Cover and cook on low for 7 to 8 hours. 3. Scoop the beef mixture into each lettuce leaf. Garnish with sesame seeds and diced scallion (if using) and serve.

Sweet Beef & Broccoli Stew

Prep Time: 15 minutes | Cook Time: 5½ to 6½ hours | Serves: 6

2 pounds boneless beef chuck roast, thinly sliced
1 cup beef broth
1 tablespoon extra-virgin olive oil
½ cup low-sodium soy sauce or coconut aminos
¼ cup coconut sugar

2 teaspoons minced garlic
¼ cup cornstarch
1 (14-ounce) bag frozen broccoli
1½ cups cooked rice

1. Put the beef in your slow cooker. 2. Whisk together the broth, soy sauce, olive oil, sugar and garlic in a medium bowl. 3. Pour the mixture over the beef and toss to coat well. Cover and cook on low for 5 to 6 hours, until the beef has cooked through. 4. Then transfer ¼ cup of the liquid to a small bowl. 5. Whisk the cornstarch to the bowl, then stir the slurry back into the ingredients in the slow cooker. 6. Stir in the broccoli. and mix well. Cover and cook for 30 minutes more. 7. Serve the beef and broccoli warm over the rice. 8. Refrigerate leftovers for up to 5 days, or freeze for up to 2 months.

BBQ Pulled Pork Sliders

Prep Time: 10 minutes | Cook Time: 8 hours | Serves: 8

4 pounds pork roast
1 teaspoon sea salt
1 teaspoon ground black pepper
1 tablespoon garlic powder
1 tablespoon chili powder
1 (32-ounce) bottle barbecue sauce

½ cup apple cider vinegar
½ cup store-bought chicken broth
1 tablespoon Worcestershire sauce
¼ cup coconut sugar
4 whole-grain buns, halved

1. Season the pork with salt, garlic powder, black pepper, and chili powder. Place the pork in the slow cooker. 2. Add the barbecue sauce, broth, Worcestershire sauce, vinegar, and sugar. Stir well. Cover and cook on low heat for 8 hours or until the pork has cooked through and can be shredded easily. 3. Then transfer the pork to a cutting board and shred it with 2 forks, then return it to the slow cooker and mix well to coat with the sauce. 4. Serve the pork warm on the buns. Refrigerate leftovers for up to 1 week, or freeze for up to 3 months.

Sweet & Spicy Pork Stew

Prep Time: 10 minutes | Cook Time: 6 hours | Serves: 8

2 tablespoons extra-virgin olive oil
1 medium yellow onion, diced
1 teaspoon garlic powder
1 teaspoon onion powder
1 teaspoon sea salt
1 teaspoon ground black pepper

¼ cup coconut sugar
1 tablespoon chili powder
1 tablespoon smoked paprika
4 pounds boneless pork loin
2 cups homemade or store-bought chicken broth

1. Combine the olive oil and onion in your slow cooker. Cook on high for 2 to 3 minutes until the onion begins to sizzle, stirring occasionally. 2. Mix together the garlic powder, onion powder, sugar, chili powder, salt, black pepper, and paprika in a small bowl. 3. Season the pork with the spice mixture and add to the slow cooker. 4. Then pour in the broth. Cover and cook on low for 6 hours or until the pork has cooked through. 5. Serve the meat warm with the broth in the bottom of the slow cooker. 6. Refrigerate leftovers for up to 1 week, or freeze for up to 3 months.

Peanut Butter Beef & Veggies Stew

Prep Time: 20 minutes | Cook Time: 8 to 10 hours | Serves: 8

3 onions, chopped
6 garlic cloves, minced
3 large carrots, shredded
2 tablespoons grated fresh ginger root
3 large tomatoes, seeded and chopped
¾ cup peanut butter

1 cup canned coconut milk
1 small red chili pepper, minced
3 tablespoons lime juice
½ cup beef stock
2½ pounds grass-fed beef sirloin roast, cut into 2-inch pieces

1. In a slow cooker, combine the carrots, onions, garlic, ginger root, and tomatoes. Stir to mix well. 2. Mix together the coconut milk, peanut butter, lime juice, chili pepper, and beef stock in a medium bowl and stir until well blended. 3. Put the roast on top of the vegetables in the slow cooker. Pour the peanut sauce over all. 4. Cover and cook on low heat for 8 to 10 hours, or until the beef is very tender.

Traditional Moroccan Beef Tagine

Prep Time: 20 minutes | Cook Time: 8 to 10 hours | Serves: 8

2 onions, chopped
6 garlic cloves, minced
2 jalapeño peppers, minced
3 carrots, cut into chunks
1 cup chopped dates

1 (3-pound) grass-fed beef sirloin roast, cut into 2-inch pieces
2 tablespoons honey
1 cup beef stock
2 teaspoons ground cumin
1 teaspoon ground turmeric

1. Combine the jalapeño peppers, onions, carrots, garlic, and dates in your slow cooker. Top with the beef. 2. Mix together the honey, cumin, beef stock, and turmeric in a small bowl. Pour into the slow cooker. 3. Cover and cook on low heat for 8 to 10 hours, or until the beef is very tender.

Italian Sausage and Peppers over Rice

Prep Time: 15 minutes | Cook Time: 6 to 7 hours | Serves: 10

2 tablespoons extra-virgin olive oil
2 pounds sweet Italian sausage links
2 red bell peppers, cored and sliced
1 orange or yellow bell pepper, cored and sliced
1 medium yellow onion, cut into strips
1 (15-ounce) jar red pasta sauce

2 teaspoons minced garlic
1 teaspoon Italian seasoning
1 teaspoon sea salt
¼ teaspoon red pepper flakes or cayenne pepper
1 to 2 cups shredded mozzarella cheese
2 to 2½ cups cooked brown or wild rice

1. Grease the bottom of the slow cooker with olive oil. Heat on low for about 2 minutes. 2. Add the sausage, bell peppers, onion, garlic, Italian seasoning, pasta sauce, salt, and red pepper flakes. Stir to mix well. Cover and cook on low for 6 to 7 hours or until the sausage has cooked through and the vegetables are soft. 3. Sprinkle with the cheese. 4. Serve warm over rice. Refrigerate leftovers for up to 1 week, or freeze for up to 2 months.

Red Wine-Braised Beef

Prep Time: 15 minutes | Cook Time: 6 to 7 hours | Serves: 6

2 tablespoons extra-virgin olive oil
2 teaspoons minced garlic
1 medium yellow onion, chopped
6 bacon slices, diced
3 cups red wine
1 cup beef broth
3 tablespoons tomato paste
½ teaspoon dried thyme
1½ cups sliced carrots

1 pound cremini mushrooms, halved
2 tablespoons dried parsley
1 or 2 bay leaves
3 pounds beef chuck roast, cut into 1- to 2-inch pieces
1 teaspoon sea salt
1 teaspoon ground black pepper
1 tablespoon cornstarch
1 tablespoon water

1. Combine the olive oil, onion, garlic, and bacon in your slow cooker. Cook on high, stirring often, for 4 to 5 minutes, until fragrant. 2. In the meantime, combine the broth, wine, and tomato paste in a large bowl. Mix well. 3. Stir the carrots, mushrooms, thyme, parsley, and bay leaf into the wine mixture. 4. Pat the beef dry and season with the salt and pepper and add to the slow cooker. 5. Pour in the wine mixture stir until well combined. 6. Then whisk in the cornstarch and water. Cover and cook on low for 6 to 7 hours, until the beef is tender and cooked through. 7. Discard the bay leaf and serve warm. 8. Refrigerate the leftovers for up to 1 week, or freeze for up to 2 months.

Parmesan Garlic Pork

Prep Time: 20 minutes | Cook Time: 7 to 9 hours | Serves: 8

2 pounds small creamer potatoes, rinsed
4 large carrots, cut into chunks
1 onion, chopped
12 garlic cloves, divided

1 (3-pound) boneless pork loin
1 cup chicken stock
1 teaspoon dried marjoram leaves
½ cup grated Parmesan cheese

1. Combine the carrots, potatoes, and onions in your slow cooker. Add half of the minced garlic to the vegetables. 2. Slice the remaining 6 cloves of garlic. Using a sharp knife, poke several holes in the pork loin and insert a garlic slice into each hole. 3. Place the pork loin on the vegetables in slow cooker. 4. Pour in the chicken stock and sprinkle with the marjoram. 5. Cover and cook on low heat for 7 to 9 hours until the pork is tender. 6. Top with the Parmesan cheese and serve.

Beef & Sweet Potato Casserole

Prep Time: 10 minutes | Cook Time: 8 to 10 hours | Serves: 6

1¾ pounds beef stew meat
2 pounds sweet potatoes, peeled and cut into 1-inch-thick pieces
1 (15-ounce) can full-fat coconut milk or coconut cream
1 onion, sliced
1 red or green bell pepper, seeded and sliced
2 carrots, peeled and chopped

4 garlic cloves, minced
2 teaspoons dried rosemary
1 teaspoon paprika
1 teaspoon salt
½ teaspoon freshly ground black pepper

1. In the slow cooker, combine all the ingredients and mix well. 2. Cover and cook on low heat for 8 to 10 hours until the potatoes are tender.

Beef & Broccoli Stew

Prep Time: 10 minutes | Cook Time: 8 to 10 hours | Serves: 4

2 pounds chuck steak, cut into thin strips
1 small onion, diced
1 cup low-sodium beef broth
½ cup low-sodium soy sauce, tamari, or coconut aminos
For the Slurry (optional):
2 tablespoons arrowroot powder

1 tablespoon toasted sesame oil
3 garlic cloves, minced
¼ teaspoon ground ginger
4 cups fresh or frozen small broccoli florets

¼ cup cold water

1. In the slow cooker, combine the beef and onion. 2. Whisk together the soy sauce, sesame oil, garlic, broth, and ginger in a medium bowl. 3. Pour the sauce into the slow cooker and stir to mix well. 4. Cover and cook on low heat for 8 to 10 hours. 5. During the last 30 minutes of cooking, add the broccoli. Re-cover and finish cooking. 6. Whisk together the arrowroot powder and water if desired. Pour the slurry into the slow cooker and stir gently. Re-cover and cook for 10 to 15 minutes longer, or until the sauce is thickened.

Juicy Beef Steak and Veggies

Prep Time: 15 minutes | Cook Time: 8 to 10 hours | Serves: 4

For the Meat:
1 onion, sliced
1 red or green bell pepper, seeded and sliced
1 (15-ounce) can corn, drained
For the Sauce:
¼ cup freshly squeezed lime juice
¼ cup freshly squeezed orange juice
3 tablespoons extra-virgin olive oil
4 garlic cloves, minced
1 teaspoon ground cumin

1 cup cooked black beans, rinsed and drained
2 pounds flank or skirt steak
Chopped fresh cilantro, for garnish

½ teaspoon chili powder
½ teaspoon dried oregano
½ teaspoon salt
¼ teaspoon freshly ground black pepper

1. In your slow cooker, combine the onion, corn, bell pepper, and black beans. 2. Top with the steak. 3. Whisk together all the sauce ingredients in a small bowl. Pour the sauce into the slow cooker, ensuring all the ingredients are covered. 4. Cover and cook on low heat for 8 to 10 hours. 5. Garnish with fresh cilantro before serving.

Beef Meat Loaf with Potatoes

Prep Time: 15 minutes | Cook Time: 8 to 10 hours | Serves: 4

For the Meat Loaf:
1 pound ground beef
1 large egg, lightly beaten
1 small onion, diced
2 garlic cloves, minced
½ cup chopped spinach
1 cup diced tomatoes
For the Ketchup:
1 (8-ounce) can tomato sauce
½ teaspoon distilled white vinegar

¼ cup almond flour
2 tablespoons Italian seasoning
1 teaspoon salt
½ teaspoon freshly ground black pepper
1-pound fingerling potatoes

1 teaspoon Italian seasoning

1. In a large bowl, mix together the ground beef, garlic, egg, onion, tomatoes, spinach, almond flour, salt, Italian seasoning, and pepper. Shape the meat mixture into a loaf. 2. Place the meatloaf in the slow cooker and arrange the potatoes around the loaf. 3. Cover and cook on low heat for 8 to 10 hours. 4. During the last 10 minutes of cooking, mix together the ketchup ingredients and spread it on top of the meat loaf. 5. Re-cover and finish cooking.

Herbed Beef Roast with Artichokes

Prep Time: 15 minutes | Cook Time: 8 to 10 hours | Serves: 6

1 pound sweet potatoes, peeled and diced
1 red or green bell pepper, seeded and sliced
1 onion, sliced
1 (3-pound) beef roast
1 (2-ounce) can sliced black olives, drained
1 (6-ounce) jar marinated artichoke hearts, with their juice
1 (15-ounce) can diced tomatoes, with their juice
3 garlic cloves, minced

1 teaspoon salt
½ teaspoon freshly ground black pepper
½ teaspoon paprika
½ teaspoon dried basil
½ teaspoon dried oregano
½ teaspoon dried parsley
¼ teaspoon red pepper flakes

1. In your slow cooker, combine the sweet potatoes, bell pepper, and onion. 2. Top with the beef roast. 3. Spread the remaining ingredients over the roast. 4. Cover and cook on low heat for 8 to 10 hours.

Tzatziki Beef Gyros

Prep Time: 10 minutes | Cook Time: 8 hours | Serves: 4

2 pounds beef chuck roast, cut into ¼-inch strips
1 large onion, halved and thinly sliced
¼ cup olive oil
2 tablespoons fresh lemon juice
2 teaspoons garlic powder
1 teaspoon dried oregano

½ teaspoon salt, plus more for seasoning
¼ teaspoon freshly ground black pepper, plus more for seasoning
Pita breads, warmed, for serving
Tzatziki sauce, for serving
Chopped lettuce and diced tomatoes, for topping (optional)

1. In your slow cooker, combine the beef and onion. 2. In a bowl, mix together the olive oil, oregano, garlic powder, lemon juice, salt, and pepper. Pour the oil mixture over the meat and toss to coat. 3. Cover and cook on low heat for 8 hours, or until the beef is tender. 4. If needed, season with more salt and pepper to taste. 5. Serve the beef and onions in pitas with tzatziki sauce. Top with lettuce and tomatoes if desired.

Sweet Beef Bolognese

Prep Time: 10 minutes | Cook Time: 7 hours | Serves: 6

2 pounds extra-lean ground beef
⅓ cup tamari or low-sodium soy sauce
2 tablespoons toasted sesame oil
2 tablespoons tomato paste
2 teaspoons minced fresh ginger

½ cup (packed) brown sugar
2 teaspoons garlic powder
½ teaspoon red pepper flakes
Chopped scallions, for garnish (optional)

1. In your slow cooker, place the beef and break it up with a wooden spoon. 2. Whisk together the tamari, sesame oil, ginger, brown sugar, tomato paste, garlic powder, and red pepper flakes. In a small bowl. Add the mixture to the beef and toss to coat. 3. Cover and cook on low heat for 7 hours. 4. Once done cooking, stir the beef mixture and break it up into smaller chunks. 5. Garnish with scallions (if using) and serve.

Savory Beef Roast and Broccoli

Prep Time: 10 minutes | Cook Time: 8 hours | Serves: 4

1 (1½-pound) beef chuck roast, cut into ¼-inch strips
½ cup tamari or low-sodium soy sauce
2 tablespoons toasted sesame oil
⅓ cup brown sugar
1 teaspoon garlic powder

2 tablespoons cornstarch
2 tablespoons water
1 (1-pound) bag frozen broccoli florets
Steamed rice, for serving (optional)

1. Place the beef strips in the slow cooker. 2. Mix together the tamari, brown sugar, sesame oil, and garlic powder in a small bowl. Pour the mixture over the beef. 3. Cover and cook on low heat for 8 hours. 4. In a bowl, whisk together the cornstarch and water. Stir the slurry into the slow cooker. Turn to high and let the sauce thicken, stirring often, uncovered. 5. Pour broccoli into a colander. Rinse broccoli with hot water until thawed. Shake colander to remove excess water. Toss broccoli into meat mixture and cook for 3 minutes to heat through. 6. Serve with rice.

Thai Beef Curry

Prep Time: 10 minutes | Cook Time: 8 hours | Serves: 6

1 (13.5-ounce) can coconut milk
⅓ cup chunky all-natural peanut butter
3 tablespoons Thai red curry paste
2 tablespoons fresh lime juice
2 tablespoons (packed) brown sugar
½ teaspoon ground ginger

½ teaspoon garlic powder
1 (1½-pound) beef chuck roast, trimmed of excess fat and cut into bite-size pieces
2 tablespoons cornstarch
2 tablespoons water

1. In your slow cooker, combine the coconut milk, curry paste, peanut butter, brown sugar, ginger, lime juice, and garlic powder. Stir until smooth and add in the beef. 2. Cover and cook on low heat for 8 hours. 3. In a small bowl, stir together the cornstarch and water. Stir the cornstarch slurry into the slow cooker. Turn to high heat and let the sauce thicken, stirring occasionally, uncovered. Serve.

Lime Shredded Beef Tacos

Prep Time: 15 minutes | Cook Time: 8 hours | Serves: 6

¼ cup beef broth
¼ cup fresh lime juice
2 tablespoons tomato paste
1 teaspoon ground cumin
1 teaspoon smoked paprika
1 teaspoon salt
½ teaspoon freshly ground black pepper

½ teaspoon garlic powder
1 medium yellow onion, finely diced
1 jalapeño pepper, seeded and minced (optional)
1 (2-pound) beef chuck roast, trimmed of excess fat
Large flour tortillas, for serving
Optional toppings: shredded cheese, sour cream, chopped tomatoes, chopped lettuce, chopped fresh cilantro

1. In your slow cooker, combine the broth, tomato paste, lime juice, paprika, cumin, salt, pepper, and garlic powder. Whisk until smooth. Add in the onion and jalapeño (if using). Then stir in the roast. 2. Cover and cook on low heat for 8 hours until the beef is tender. 3. Transfer the beef to a cutting board, using two forks to shred the beef. Return the beef to the slow cooker and stir well. 4. Serve the beef on tortillas and your favorite taco toppings.

Spiced Flank Steak Fajitas

Prep Time: 15 minutes | Cook Time: 8 hours | Serves: 5

2 medium yellow onions, halved and thinly sliced
2 teaspoons olive oil
2 bell peppers (any color), seeded and sliced lengthwise
1 cup salsa
1 (1½-pound) flank steak, trimmed of excess fat
1 teaspoon ground cumin
1 teaspoon chili powder

½ teaspoon garlic powder
½ teaspoon onion powder
½ teaspoon salt
¼ teaspoon freshly ground black pepper
5 (8-inch) flour tortillas
Optional toppings: shredded cheese, sour cream, guacamole, pico de gallo, chopped fresh cilantro

1. Place the onions in your slow cooker and drizzle with olive oil. Add the bell peppers. Pour salsa over them. 2. Top with the steak and sprinkle the steak with the cumin, garlic powder, onion powder, chili powder, salt, and pepper. 3. Cover and cook on low heat for 8 hours. 4. Transfer the beef to a cutting board and tent loosely with aluminum foil and let it rest for 10 minutes. Slice into thin strips. 5. Serve the beef on top of the tortillas, and spoon the onions and bell peppers over the beef. 6. Serve with the toppings you like.

Beef Pepperoncini Sandwiches

Prep Time: 10 minutes | Cook Time: 8 hours | Serves: 8

4 pounds eye of round boneless roast, trimmed of fat
1 (16-ounce) jar pepperoncini, with all but ¼ cup of their liquid

8 French sub buns, sliced

1. Place the beef roast in the slow cooker. Top with the pepperoncini and the liquid. Cover and cook on low heat for 8 hours. 2. Use two forks to shred the meat and return it to the slow cooker. 3. Drizzle some of the juice on the inside of the bun before chucking in the shredded beef. Serve immediately.

Chapter 5 Fish and Seafood

Nutritious Manhattan-Style Clam Chowder

Prep Time: 15 minutes | Cook Time: 8 hours | Serves: 4

½ tablespoon extra-virgin olive oil
½ medium yellow onion, finely chopped
1 large carrot, finely chopped
1 celery rib, finely chopped
½ pound small red potatoes, diced
3 tablespoons chili sauce
1 tablespoon tomato paste
½ tablespoon gluten-free Worcestershire sauce

½ teaspoon dried thyme
½ teaspoon hot sauce
1 (15-ounce) can no-salt-added diced tomatoes, with their juices
1 (8-ounce) bottle clam juice
1 bay leaf
2 (6½-ounce) cans chopped clams, drained
2 tablespoons chopped fresh parsley

1. In a 6-quart slow cooker, combine the oil, onion, carrot, celery, potatoes, chili sauce, tomato paste, Worcestershire sauce, thyme, hot sauce, tomatoes with their juices, and clam juice. Add the bay leaf. 2. Cover and cook on low for 6 to 8 hours, until the potatoes are fork-tender. 3. When finished, remove and discard the bay leaf and stir in the clams. Cover and allow the pot to sit for 5 minutes. 4. Ladle into serving bowls and garnish with the parsley. 5. Refrigerate leftovers for up to 4 days or freeze for up to 6 months.

Sweet and Sour Scallops with Pineapples

Prep Time: 10 minutes | Cook Time: 4 hours 10 minutes | Serves: 4

1 (8-ounce) can pineapple chunks, packed in juice
¼ cup rice vinegar, white vinegar, or apple cider vinegar
⅓ cup no-salt-added ketchup
1 tablespoon low-sodium gluten-free tamari or soy sauce
1 tablespoon light brown sugar
1 teaspoon minced fresh ginger

1 tablespoon minced garlic
2 medium bell peppers (any color), cut into 1-inch pieces
1 small sweet onion, cut into 1-inch pieces
1 pound sea scallops
Cauliflower rice or brown rice, cooked, for serving (optional)
Thinly sliced scallions, green and white parts, for garnish

1. Drain the pineapple chunks, reserving ¼ cup of the juice. Pour the reserved juice into a 6-quart slow cooker. Whisk in the vinegar, ketchup, tamari, brown sugar, ginger, and garlic. Add the pineapple chunks, bell peppers, and onion. 2. Cover and cook on low for 4 hours, until the vegetables are crisp-tender. 3. Stir in the scallops. Cover and cook on low for 8 to 10 minutes, or until the scallops are barely opaque. (Don't overcook them or they will become rubbery.) 4. Divide the rice (if using) among serving bowls. Top with the scallop mixture and scallions. 5. Refrigerate leftovers for up to 4 days or freeze for up to 3 months.

Lemony Rosemary Salmon Steaks

Prep Time: 10 minutes | Cook Time: 2 hours | Serves: 2

2 salmon steaks, about 1" thick each
⅓ cup white wine
2 tablespoons lemon juice
4 thin slices fresh lemon

1 tablespoon nonpareil capers
½ teaspoon minced fresh rosemary
½ teaspoon kosher salt

1. Place the salmon on the bottom of a 2- or 4-quart slow cooker. Add the wine and lemon juice over the fish. Place the lemon slices in a single layer on top of the fish. Sprinkle with capers, rosemary, and salt. 2. Cook on low for 2 hours. 3. When finished, discard lemon slices prior to serving.

Indian Tikka Masala Sloppy Joe Sliders

Prep Time: 10 minutes | Cook Time: 8 hours | Serves: 8

2 pounds ground turkey or chicken
¼ cup white wine vinegar
1 small red onion, finely chopped
1 cup tikka masala sauce

½ teaspoon garam masala or ground cumin
8 small whole-grain rolls (halved) or slider buns, for serving
Sliced cucumbers, for serving
Plain low-fat yogurt, for serving

1. In a 6-quart slow cooker, combine the turkey, vinegar, onion, tikka masala sauce, and garam masala. 2. Cover and cook on low for 6 to 8 hours, until the turkey is cooked through and the flavors have melded. 3. Place the opened rolls on serving plates. Cover the bottom of each roll with cucumber slices and spoon the turkey mixture on top. Drizzle with yogurt, top with the other half of each roll, and serve immediately. 4. Refrigerate leftovers for up to 4 days or freeze for up to 3 months.

Healthy Sea Bass with Mango Salsa

Prep Time: 10 minutes | Cook Time: 4 hours | Serves: 4

Cooking spray
4 sea bass fillets
2 tablespoons olive oil, divided
1 ripe mango, peeled and finely diced
¼ cup finely diced red onion

1 baby red pepper, finely chopped (optional)
6–8 sprigs cilantro leaves, finely chopped
1 tablespoon fresh lime juice
¼ teaspoon kosher salt
¼ teaspoon coarsely ground black pepper

1. Lightly coat the inside of a 4-quart slow cooker with cooking spray. Arrange fillets in a single layer on the bottom of the cooker. Drizzle 1 tablespoon of the olive oil over the fillets. 2. Cook on low for 3–4 hours or until fish flakes easily with a fork. 3. Meanwhile, mix the remaining olive oil with the remaining ingredients in a small mixing bowl. Refrigerate until ready to use. 4. Carefully lift cooked fillets onto a serving platter. Spoon mango salsa over fillets and serve immediately.

Garlic Sea Bass with Tofu

Prep Time: 10 minutes | Cook Time: 4 hours | Serves: 4

Cooking spray
4 sea bass fillets
1 tablespoon olive oil
2 garlic cloves, minced
1 teaspoon ground ginger
2 tablespoons black bean and garlic sauce

2 tablespoons soy sauce
1 teaspoon granulated sugar
⅛ teaspoon black pepper
8 ounces extra-firm tofu, drained and diced
3–4 scallions, green parts thinly sliced for garnish

1. Lightly coat the inside of a 4-quart slow cooker with cooking spray. Arrange fillets in a single layer on the bottom of the cooker. 2. Whisk together the oil, garlic, ginger, black bean and garlic sauce, soy sauce, sugar, and black pepper in a medium bowl. Use a spoon to gently mix in the tofu. Pour over the fish. Cook on low for 3–4 hours or until fish flakes easily with a fork. Transfer the fish to the covered dish; keep warm. 3. Increase the heat to high and cook the sauce uncovered for 15 minutes. Serve fish with the sauce, garnished with the sliced scallions if desired.

Lemony Mustard Poached Salmon

Prep Time: 10 minutes | Cook Time: 4 hours | Serves: 4

1 tablespoon unsalted butter
4 thin slices sweet onion
2 cups water
4 (6-ounce) salmon steaks
Kosher salt, to taste
1 lemon

2 tablespoons extra-virgin olive oil
2 teaspoons fresh lemon juice
½ teaspoon Dijon mustard
Freshly ground white or black pepper, to taste (optional)
1 tablespoon fresh flat leaf parsley leaves, minced

1. Use the butter to grease the bottom and halfway up the sides of the slow cooker. Arrange the onion slices over the bottom of the slow cooker, pressing them into the butter so that they stay in place. Pour in the water. Cover and cook on high for 30 minutes. 2. Place a salmon steak over each onion slice. Salt to taste. Thinly slice the lemon; discard the seeds and place the slices over the fish. Cover and cook on high for 45 minutes or until the fish is opaque. 3. Transfer the (well-drained) fish to individual serving plates or to a serving platter. 4. Add the oil, lemon juice, mustard, and white or black pepper in a small bowl, if using; whisk to combine. Immediately before serving the salmon, fold in the parsley. Evenly divide the sauce among the salmon steaks.

Light Tuna Corn Chowder

Prep Time: 10 minutes | Cook Time: 4-6 hours | Serves: 4

2 (5-ounce) cans solid white tuna packed in water, undrained
4 medium potatoes, peeled and cut into ½" chunks
1 small onion, peeled and diced
1 (20-ounce) bag frozen corn, defrosted
3 cups water, heated to a simmer
2 teaspoons kosher salt, plus more to taste

¼ teaspoon ground black pepper, plus more to taste
1 (12-ounce) can evaporated milk
½ cup frozen peas and carrots, defrosted
¼ cup dry sherry (optional)
¼ cup chopped Italian parsley leaves (for garnish)
¼ cup imitation bacon chips, such as Bacos (for garnish)

1. Place the tuna in a 4-quart slow cooker. Break up the tuna with a fork. Stir in the potatoes, onion, corn, and water. Cover and cook on low for 4–6 hours. 2. Stir in the salt, pepper, evaporated milk, peas, carrots, and the sherry if using. Cover and cook on low for an additional 30 minutes. Taste and add additional salt and pepper if needed. 3. Garnish with the parsley leaves and imitation bacon chips, if using, before serving.

Tasty Tuna with Garlic Butter in Foil

Prep Time: 10 minutes | Cook Time: 2 hours | Serves: 8

½ cup (1 stick) unsalted butter, softened
4 minced garlic cloves
1 teaspoon salt
2 tablespoons minced fresh Italian parsley leaves

Cooking spray
8 (6-ounce) tuna steaks
1 lemon, thinly sliced

1. Whisk together butter, garlic, salt, and parsley in a small bowl. Set aside. 2. Lightly spray 8 large pieces of aluminum foil with cooking spray. Place 1 tuna steak on each piece of foil. Divide the butter mixture evenly and spread over the tuna steaks. Top with the lemon slices. Fold up two edges and crimp together, allowing a little space for steam to expand. Fold up the ends and crimp together as well. 3. Place packets in a 6-quart slow cooker. Cook on high for 2 hours. 4. When finished, serve.

Flavorful Seafood Stew

Prep Time: 15 minutes | Cook Time: 6 to 7 hours | Serves: 6

1 (28-ounce) can crushed tomatoes
3 cups savory vegetable broth or store-bought vegetable broth
1 (8-ounce) can clam juice
¼ cup white-wine vinegar
¼ cup water
4 teaspoons minced garlic
3½ cups chopped and peeled baby potatoes
1 small yellow onion, diced

1 teaspoon dried basil
1 teaspoon dried cilantro
1 teaspoon dried thyme
1 teaspoon sea salt
½ teaspoon ground black pepper
¼ teaspoon red pepper flakes
2 pounds frozen seafood mix, thawed

1. Combine the tomatoes, broth, vinegar, clam juice, water, garlic, onion, potatoes, basil, cilantro, salt, black pepper, thyme, and red pepper flakes in your slow cooker. Cover and cook on low for 6 hours or until the potatoes are very tender. 2. Stir in the thawed seafood mix. Cover and cook on high for 30 minutes to 1 hour or until the seafood is cooked through. 3. Serve the stew warm. Refrigerate leftovers for up to 5 days, or freeze for up to 1 month.

Fresh White Fish with Curried Tomato Sauce

Prep Time: 20 minutes | Cook Time: 4 hours | Serves: 6

2 tablespoons extra-virgin olive oil
1 medium yellow or sweet onion, finely chopped
2 garlic cloves, minced
1 (½-inch) piece fresh ginger, peeled and grated
2 (14½-ounce) cans no-salt-added diced fire-roasted tomatoes, with their juices
¼ teaspoon kosher salt

¼ teaspoon ground black pepper
¼ teaspoon ground cayenne pepper
1 teaspoon curry powder
4 cups stemmed and chopped Tuscan kale
2 pounds firm white fish, such as cod, halibut, or haddock, cut into 3-inch pieces
Fresh chopped parsley, for garnish

1. Preheat a 6-quart slow cooker for 20 minutes on low. In the slow cooker, combine the oil, yellow onion, garlic, ginger, tomatoes with their juices, salt, black pepper, cayenne pepper, and curry powder. 2. Cover and cook on low heat for 4 hours, until hot and bubbly. 3. Add the kale and stir well. Nestle the fish into the sauce. 4. Cover and cook on high for 25 to 30 minutes, until the fish flakes easily with a fork or reaches an internal temperature of 145°F. 5. Spoon into serving bowls and sprinkle with parsley. Serve immediately. 6. Refrigerate the leftovers for up to 4 days or freeze for up to 6 months.

Garlic Vegetable Shrimp Scampi

Prep Time: 20 minutes | Cook Time: 5½ to 7½ hours | Serves: 8

1 pound cremini mushrooms, sliced
2 onions, chopped
2 leeks, chopped
8 garlic cloves, minced
1 cup fish stock

¼ cup freshly squeezed lemon juice
1 teaspoon dried basil leaves
2 pounds raw shrimp, shelled and deveined
2 tablespoons butter

1. Combine the onions, mushrooms, leeks, garlic, lemon juice, fish stock, and basil. Cover and cook on low for 5 to 7 hours until the vegetables are tender. 2. Add the shrimp and stir well. Cover and cook on high heat for 30 to 40 minutes until the shrimp curl and turn pink. 3. Add in the butter and stir to mix well; cover and let rest for 10 minutes, then serve.

Cheesy Salmon and Pasta Casserole

Prep Time: 15 minutes | Cook Time: 4½ to 6 hours | Serves: 6

1 tablespoon extra-virgin olive oil
1 tablespoon minced garlic
1 pound cremini mushrooms, sliced
1 medium yellow onion, diced
1 red bell pepper, cored and diced
6 cups baby spinach (about 5 ounces)
1 (15-ounce) container ricotta cheese
1 large egg
2 cups shredded mozzarella cheese, divided

½ cup grated Parmesan cheese, divided
2 (24-ounce) jars no-sugar-added red pasta sauce of your choice, divided
1 pound whole-grain penne, divided
1 pound wild-caught salmon fillets (3 or 4 fillets)
½ lemon
Sea salt
Ground black pepper

1. Combine the olive oil, garlic, onion, mushrooms, and bell pepper in the slow cooker. Cook on high for 2 to 3 minutes. 2. Add in the spinach, 1 cup at a time, allowing it to wilt a bit. Stir well. 3. In a large bowl, whisk together the egg, 1 cup of mozzarella cheese, ricotta cheese, and ¼ cup of Parmesan cheese. 4. Pour half of the vegetable mixture from the slow cooker into another large bowl. 5. Pour 1 cup of pasta sauce over the remaining vegetables in the slow cooker. 6. Arrange half of the penne in a layer over the sauce, then layer, in order, 2 cups of pasta sauce, half of the ricotta mixture, and half of the vegetable mixture in the bowl. Repeat this layering step one more time. Cover and cook on low heat for 4 to 5 hours, until the noodles are cooked through and the vegetables are tender. 7. Sprinkle the remaining 1 cup of mozzarella cheese and ¼ cup of Parmesan cheese on the pasta and vegetables. 8. Lay the salmon fillets flat on top of cheese, then squeeze the lemon lightly over the fillets. 9. Pour the remaining 1 cup pasta sauce over the salmon. 10. Cover and cook for 30 minutes to 1 hour longer or until the salmon is cooked through. 11. Season with salt and pepper and serve warm. 12. Refrigerate leftovers for up to 5 days, or freeze for up to 1 month.

Parmesan Salmon and Barley Stew

Prep Time: 20 minutes | Cook Time: 7½ to 8½ hours | Serves: 6

2 cups hulled barley, rinsed
2 fennel bulbs, cored and chopped
2 red bell peppers, stemmed, seeded, and chopped
4 garlic cloves, minced
1 (8-ounce) package cremini mushrooms, sliced

5 cups roasted vegetable broth
1 teaspoon dried tarragon leaves
⅛ teaspoon freshly ground black pepper
6 (5-ounce) salmon fillets
⅓ cup grated Parmesan cheese

1. Mix together the barley, bell peppers, garlic, fennel, mushrooms, tarragon, vegetable broth, and pepper in your slow cooker. Cover and cook on low heat for 7 to 8 hours, until most of the liquid is absorbed and the vegetables are tender. 2. Arrange the salmon fillets on top of the barley mixture. Cover the lid and cook on low for 20 to 40 minutes, or until the salmon flakes are fork-tender. 3. Stir in the Parmesan cheese, breaking up the salmon, and serve.

Homemade Salmon Ratatouille

Prep Time: 10 minutes | Cook Time: 6½ to 7½ hours | Serves: 8

2 eggplants, peeled and chopped
5 large tomatoes, seeded and chopped
2 cups sliced button mushrooms
2 onions, chopped
2 red bell peppers, stemmed, seeded, and chopped

5 garlic cloves, minced
2 tablespoons olive oil
1 teaspoon dried herbes de Provence
2 pounds salmon fillets

1. In the slow cooker, combine the onions, bell peppers, eggplant, mushrooms, tomatoes, olive oil, garlic, and herbes de Provence. Cover and cook on low for 6 to 7 hours, until the vegetables are tender. 2. Add the salmon. Cover and cook on low for 30 to 40 minutes longer until the salmon flakes are fork-tender. 3. Gently stir and serve.

Shrimp and Chicken Casserole

Prep Time: 20 minutes | Cook Time: 7½ to 9½ hours | Serves: 8

10 (4-ounce) boneless, skinless chicken thighs, cut into 2-inch pieces
2 onions, chopped
6 garlic cloves, minced
2 jalapeño peppers, minced
2 green bell peppers, stemmed, seeded, and chopped

5 celery stalks, sliced
2 cups chicken stock
1 tablespoon Cajun seasoning
¼ teaspoon cayenne pepper
1½ pounds raw shrimp, shelled and deveined

1. Combine the chicken, garlic, onions, celery, chicken stock, jalapeños, bell peppers, Cajun seasoning, and cayenne in your slow cooker. Cover and cook on low for 7 to 9 hours until the internal temperature of the chicken registers 165°F on a food thermometer. 2. Add the shrimp and stir well. Cover and cook for 30 to 40 minutes longer, or until the shrimp curl and turn pink. Serve warm.

Cheesy Shrimp and Grits

Prep Time: 10 minutes | Cook Time: 5½ to 7½ hours | Serves: 8

2½ cups stone-ground grits
2 onions, chopped
5 garlic cloves, minced
4 large tomatoes, seeded and chopped
2 green bell peppers, stemmed, seeded, and chopped

8 cups chicken stock or Roasted vegetable broth
1 bay leaf
1 teaspoon Old Bay seasoning
2 pounds raw shrimp, peeled and deveined
1½ cups shredded Cheddar cheese

1. Combine the grits, onions, garlic, bell peppers, tomatoes, bay leaf, chicken stock, and seasoning in your slow cooker. Cover and cook on low for 5 to 7 hours until the grits are soft and most of the liquid is absorbed. 2. Stir in the shrimp. Cover and cook on low for 30 to 40 minutes more, or until the shrimp curl and turn pink. 3. Stir in the cheese and serve.

Delicious Seafood Bouillabaisse

Prep Time: 10 minutes | Cook Time: 4□ to 5¼ hours | Serves: 6

1 tablespoon extra-virgin olive oil
¼ cup tomato paste
1 (15-ounce) can no-salt-added crushed tomatoes, with their juices
4 cups no-salt-added vegetable broth or seafood stock
1 large fennel bulb, cut into 8 wedges, feathery fronds reserved and chopped

3 tablespoons minced garlic
3 bay leaves
2 (6-ounce) cans chopped clams, drained
2 pounds cod, monkfish, halibut, or haddock fillets, cut into 2-inch pieces
Grated zest from 1 small orange

1. Combine the oil, tomatoes with their juices, tomato paste, and vegetable stock in your slow cooker. Add the garlic, fennel wedges, and bay leaves. 2. Cover and cook on low heat for 4½ to 5 hours, or until the fennel is tender and the mixture is hot and bubbly. 3. Stir in the clams. Nestle the fish in the sauce and cook on low for 15 to 20 minutes longer, until the fish is opaque and the internal temperature reaches 145°F. Remove and discard the bay leaves. 4. Ladle the bouillabaisse into serving bowls and garnish with the reserved fennel fronds and orange zest. 5. Refrigerate leftovers for up to 4 days or freeze for up to 6 months.

White Wine-Braised Mussels

Prep Time: 10 minutes | Cook Time: 6¼ to 8¼ hours | Serves: 6

½ tablespoon extra-virgin olive oil
1 tablespoon minced garlic
1½ cups marinara sauce with red lentils or store-bought low-sugar, low-sodium marinara sauce
2½ cups no-salt-added vegetable broth or water
1 cup dry white wine

2 tablespoons Italian seasoning
¾ teaspoon garlic pepper or ground black pepper
¼ teaspoon red pepper flakes (optional)
2 pounds live mussels, scrubbed and debearded
Chopped fresh parsley, for garnish

1. In your slow cooker, mix together the oil, marinara sauce, garlic, vegetable broth, garlic pepper, Italian seasoning, wine, and red pepper flakes (if using). 2. Cover and cook on low heat for 6 to 8 hours, or until the flavors have melded and the sauce is bubbling. 3. Stir in the mussels and cook on high for 15 to 20 minutes longer, until the mussels open. Discard any mussels that don't open. 4. Using a large spoon, place the mussels in a large bowl. Pour the sauce over the mussels and garnish with the parsley. 5. Refrigerate leftovers for up to 4 days or freeze for up to 3 months.

Chapter 6 Soup, Chili and Stew

Heart-Healthy Apple-Parsnip Soup

Prep Time: 10 minutes | Cook Time: 7-8 hours | Serves: 6-8

6 parsnips (about 2 pounds), peeled and cut into chunks
5 large Granny Smith apples, peeled, cored, and quartered
4 cups vegetable broth
4 cups water
1 (15-ounce) can cannellini beans, drained and rinsed, or 1½ to 2 cups great northern beans

1 Vidalia onion, finely chopped
1 large red bell pepper, chopped
6 garlic cloves, minced
1 tablespoon curry powder
Freshly ground black pepper
Extra-virgin olive oil, for garnish

1. Add the parsnips, apples, broth, water, beans, onion, bell pepper, garlic, curry powder, and pepper to a 6-quart slow cooker and stir to combine. Cover and cook on low for 7 to 8 hours, until the parsnips are tender. 2. Using an immersion blender, purée the soup until smooth. 3. When finished, serve immediately with a drizzle of olive oil as a garnish, if desired.

Classic Yummy Jambalaya Soup

Prep Time: 15 minutes | Cook Time: 6-7 hours | Serves: 8

1 tablespoon extra-virgin olive oil
6 cups chicken broth
1 (28-ounce) can diced tomatoes
1 pound spicy organic sausage, sliced
1 cup chopped cooked chicken
1 red bell pepper, chopped
½ sweet onion, chopped

1 jalapeño pepper, chopped
2 teaspoons minced garlic
3 tablespoons cajun seasoning
½ pound medium shrimp, peeled, deveined, and chopped
½ cup sour cream, for garnish
1 avocado, diced, for garnish
2 tablespoons chopped cilantro, for garnish

1. Lightly grease the insert of the slow cooker with the olive oil. 2. Add the broth, tomatoes, sausage, chicken, red bell pepper, onion, jalapeño pepper, garlic, and cajun seasoning. 3. Cover and cook on low for 6 to 7 hours. 4. Stir in the shrimp and leave on low for 30 minutes, or until the shrimp are cooked through. 5. Serve topped with the sour cream, avocado, and cilantro.

Easy Chicken-Vegetable Soup

Prep Time: 15 minutes | Cook Time: 7-8 hours | Serves: 6

1 tablespoon extra-virgin olive oil
4 cups chicken broth
2 cups coconut milk
2 cups diced chicken breast
½ sweet onion, chopped
2 celery stalks, chopped

1 carrot, diced
½ cup chopped cauliflower
2 teaspoons minced garlic
1 teaspoon chopped thyme
1 teaspoon chopped oregano
¼ teaspoon freshly ground black pepper

1. Lightly grease the insert of the slow cooker with the olive oil. 2. Add the broth, coconut milk, chicken, onion, celery, carrot, cauliflower, garlic, thyme, oregano, and pepper. 3. Cover and cook on low for 7 to 8 hours. 4. Serve warm.

Tender Beef Stew

Prep Time: 15 minutes | Cook Time: 8 hours | Serves: 6

3 tablespoons extra-virgin olive oil, divided
1 (2-pound) beef chuck roast, cut into 1-inch chunks
½ teaspoon salt
¼ teaspoon freshly ground black pepper
2 cups beef broth
1 cup diced tomatoes

¼ cup apple cider vinegar
1½ cups cubed pumpkin, cut into 1-inch chunks
½ sweet onion, chopped
2 teaspoons minced garlic
1 teaspoon dried thyme
1 tablespoon chopped fresh parsley, for garnish

1. Lightly grease the insert of the slow cooker with 1 tablespoon of the olive oil. 2. Lightly season the beef chucks with the salt and pepper. 3. In a large skillet over medium-high heat, warm the remaining 2 tablespoons of the olive oil. add the beef and brown on all sides, about 7 minutes. 4. Transfer the beef to the insert and stir in the broth, tomatoes, apple cider vinegar, pumpkin, onion, garlic, and thyme. 5. Cover and cook on low heat for about 8 hours, until the beef is very tender. 6. Serve topped with the parsley.

Juicy Creamy Chicken Stew

Prep Time: 20 minutes | Cook Time: 6 hours | Serves: 6

3 tablespoons extra-virgin olive oil, divided
1 pound boneless chicken thighs, diced into 1½-inch pieces
½ sweet onion, chopped
2 teaspoons minced garlic
2 cups chicken broth
2 celery stalks, diced

1 carrot, diced
1 teaspoon dried thyme
1 cup shredded kale
1 cup coconut cream
Salt, for seasoning
Freshly ground black pepper, for seasoning

1. Lightly grease the insert of the slow cooker with 1 tablespoon of the olive oil. 2. In a large skillet over medium-high heat, warm the remaining 2 tablespoons of the olive oil. add the chicken and sauté until it is just cooked through, about 7 minutes. 3. Place in the onion and garlic and sauté for another 3 minutes. 4. Transfer the chicken mixture to the insert, and stir in the broth, celery, carrot, and thyme. 5. Cover and cook on low for 6 hours. 6. Stir in the kale and coconut cream. 7. Season with the salt and pepper, and serve warm.

Homemade Chicken Bone Broth

Prep Time: 15 minutes | Cook Time: 24 hours | Serves: 8 cups

1 tablespoon extra-virgin olive oil
2 chicken carcasses, separated into pieces
2 garlic cloves, crushed
1 celery stalk, chopped
1 carrot, chopped

½ sweet onion, cut into eighths
2 tablespoons apple cider vinegar
2 bay leaves
½ teaspoon black peppercorns
Water

1. Lightly grease the insert of the slow cooker with the olive oil. 2. Place the chicken bones, garlic, celery, carrot, onion, apple cider vinegar, bay leaves, and peppercorns in the insert. add water until the liquid reaches about 1½ inches from the top of the insert. 3. Cover and cook on low for about 24 hours. 4. Strain the broth through a fine-mesh cheesecloth and throw away the solids. 5. Store the broth in sealed containers in the refrigerator for up to 5 days or in the freezer for up to 1 month.

Perfect Herbed Vegetable Broth

Prep Time: 15 minutes | Cook Time: 8 hours | Serves: 8 cups

1 tablespoon extra-virgin olive oil
4 garlic cloves, crushed
2 celery stalks with greens, roughly chopped
1 sweet onion, quartered
1 carrot, roughly chopped
½ cup chopped parsley

4 thyme sprigs
2 bay leaves
½ teaspoon black peppercorns
½ teaspoon salt
8 cups water

1. Lightly grease the insert of the slow cooker with the olive oil. 2. Place the garlic, celery, onion, carrot, parsley, thyme, bay leaves, peppercorns, and salt in the insert. add the water. 3. Cover and cook on low for about 8 hours. 4. Strain the broth through a fine-mesh cheesecloth and throw away the solids. 5. Store the broth in sealed containers in the refrigerator for up to 5 days or in the freezer for up to 1 month.

Thick Beef Bone Broth

Prep Time: 15 minutes | Cook Time: 24 hours | Serves: 8 cups

1 tablespoon extra-virgin olive oil
2 pounds beef bones with marrow
2 celery stalks with greens, chopped
1 carrot, roughly chopped
1 sweet onion, quartered
4 garlic cloves, crushed
2 tablespoons apple cider vinegar

½ teaspoon whole black peppercorns
½ teaspoon salt
2 bay leaves
5 parsley sprigs
4 thyme sprigs
Water

1. Lightly grease the insert of the slow cooker with the olive oil. 2. Place the beef bones, celery, carrot, onion, garlic, apple cider vinegar, peppercorns, salt, bay leaves, parsley, and thyme in the insert. add water until the liquid reaches about 1½ inches from the top. 3. Cover and cook on low for about 24 hours. 4. Strain the broth through a fine-mesh cheesecloth and throw away the solids. 5. Store the broth in sealed containers in the refrigerator for up to 5 days or in the freezer for up to 1 month.

Simple Rustic Italian Chicken Stew

Prep Time: 15 minutes | Cook Time: 7 hours | Serves: 4

¼ cup extra-virgin olive oil
12 ounces whole chicken legs and thighs
1 cup chicken broth
1 cup pitted green or black olives
1 stalk celery, chopped
½ onion, diced
2 garlic cloves, minced

2 tablespoons dry white wine
1 tablespoon tomato paste
1 teaspoon fennel seeds, crushed
½ teaspoon kosher salt
1 cup heavy (whipping) cream
2 tablespoons chopped fresh parsley

1. Combine the olive oil, chicken, chicken broth, olives, celery, onion, garlic, white wine, tomato paste, fennel seeds, and salt in the slow cooker. Stir to mix. Cover and cook for 7 hours on low. 2. Just before serving, stir in the heavy cream and the parsley.

Yummy Condensed Cream of Mushroom Soup

Prep Time: 15 minutes | Cook Time: 4 hours | Serves: 3 cups

½ cup (1 stick) unsalted butter or ghee
1 medium onion, chopped
2 garlic cloves, minced
1 pound sliced mushrooms
1 cup dry white wine
2 cups vegetable broth

1 fresh thyme sprig
1½ teaspoons kosher salt
1½ teaspoons freshly ground black pepper
4 ounces cream cheese
¾ cup heavy (whipping) cream

1. Melt the butter over medium-high heat in a large skillet. Add the onion and garlic and sauté until softened, about 5 minutes. 2. Add the mushrooms and sauté until softened, about 3 minutes more. 3. Stir in the white wine, bring to a boil, and cook for 2 more minutes. Transfer the vegetables to the slow cooker. 4. Stir in the vegetable broth, salt, thyme, and pepper. Cover and cook for 4 hours on low or 2 hours on high. 5. When finished, discard the thyme sprig and use an immersion blender or a countertop blender to purée the soup (half or all of it). 6. Stir in the heavy cream and cream cheese. Use immediately or transfer to jars and keep refrigerated for up to 1 week.

Tomato Chicken & Sausage Gumbo

Prep Time: 10 minutes | Cook Time: 7 hours | Serves: 6

1½ pounds andouille sausage or other spicy smoked sausage, halved lengthwise and sliced crosswise
1 pound boneless, skinless chicken thighs, diced
1 (28-ounce) can diced tomatoes, with juice
2 cups chicken broth
1 (10-ounce) package frozen sliced okra, thawed
2 celery stalks, diced
1 green bell pepper, seeded and diced
1 onion, diced

3 garlic cloves, minced
2 bay leaves
1 teaspoon dried thyme
1 teaspoon dried oregano
½ teaspoon ground mustard
½ teaspoon kosher salt
¼ teaspoon freshly ground black pepper
¼ teaspoon cayenne pepper
4 scallions, thinly sliced

1. In the slow cooker, combine the sausage, chicken, tomatoes and their juice, chicken broth, okra, celery, green bell pepper, onion, garlic, bay leaves, thyme, oregano, ground mustard, salt, black pepper, and cayenne pepper. Stir to mix. Cover and cook for 7 hours on low. 2. When finished, discard the bay leaves and serve hot, garnished with the scallions.

Traditional Scotch Broth

Prep Time: 10 minutes | Cook Time: 6-8 hours | Serves: 4

2 leeks, white part only
4 lamb shoulder chops
⅓ cup pearl barley
1 large carrot, peeled and diced
1 stalk of celery, thinly sliced

2 medium potatoes, peeled and diced
6 cups water
Salt and freshly ground black pepper, to taste
Fresh parsley, minced (optional)

1. Dice the white part of the leeks; rinse well and drain. Add the leeks to the slow cooker along with the lamb chops, barley, carrot, celery, potatoes, water, salt, and pepper. Cover and cook on low for 6–8 hours or until the meat is tender and the potatoes are cooked through. 2. When finished, transfer a lamb chop to each of 4 bowls and ladle the soup over the meat. Garnish with the parsley if desired.

Herbed Green Split Pea Soup

Prep Time: 10 minutes | Cook Time: 6-8 hours | Serves: 6

2 cups dried green split peas
Water, as needed
6 cups homemade or store-bought vegetable broth
2 medium potatoes, peeled and diced
2 large carrots, chopped
3 stalks celery, chopped

2 cloves garlic, minced
1 teaspoon cumin
1 teaspoon thyme
1 bay leaf
1 teaspoon salt

1. Rinse the green split peas; soak overnight in enough water to cover them by more than 1". Drain. 2. In a 4-quart slow cooker, add all ingredients and cook on low heat for 6–8 hours. 3. Let the soup cool slightly, then remove the bay leaf. Process in a blender, or use an immersion blender, until smooth.

Creamy Cheeseburger Soup

Prep Time: 10 minutes | Cook Time: 6-8 hours | Serves: 6

1 pound 93% lean ground beef
4 cups low-sodium beef broth
1 small onion, diced
2 cloves garlic, minced
1 (15-ounce) can low-sodium or no-salt-added diced tomatoes
2 tablespoons Dijon mustard
2 tablespoons Worcestershire sauce

1 teaspoon dried parsley
½ teaspoon salt
¼ teaspoon freshly ground black pepper
1½ cups shredded Cheddar cheese
1 cup reduced-fat 2% milk
6 ounces bacon, cooked and crumbled

1. Add the beef, broth, onion, garlic, tomatoes, mustard, parsley, salt, Worcestershire sauce, and pepper to the slow cooker. Stir to mix well. 2. Cook on low for 6 to 8 hours or on high for 3 to 4 hours. 3. Stir in the cheese and the milk, and cook on high heat for 1 additional hour. 4. Top with the bacon before serving.

Savory Zuppa Toscana with Cauliflower

Prep Time: 10 minutes | Cook Time: 4-6 hours | Serves: 6

1 pound Italian sausage
1 tablespoon extra-virgin olive oil
1 small onion, diced
3 garlic cloves, minced
4½ cups low-sodium chicken broth
1 large head cauliflower, cut into small florets

3 cups chopped kale
1 teaspoon salt
½ teaspoon freshly ground black pepper
¼ teaspoon red pepper flakes
½ cup heavy (whipping) cream

1. Add the sausage, olive oil, onion, garlic, broth, cauliflower, kale, salt, black pepper, and red pepper flakes to the slow cooker. Stir to mix well. 2. Cook on low for 4 to 6 hours or on high for 2 to 3 hours. 3. Stir in the cream and serve.

Delicious Moose Soup

Prep Time: 10 minutes | Cook Time: 4-6 hours | Serves: 6

2 carrots, peeled and cut into ¼" slices
2 parsnips, peeled and cut into ¼" slices
3 tablespoons vegetable oil
2 pounds moose (or beef stew) meat, diced
1 large onion, finely diced
1 jalapeño pepper, minced
1 rib celery, diced

2 cloves garlic, minced
10 cups water or beef broth
1 (16-ounce) can diced tomatoes, drained
2 cups cooked wild rice
1 teaspoon kosher salt, or to taste
¼ teaspoon black pepper, or to taste

1. Add the carrots and parsnips into a 4- or 6-quart slow cooker. Set aside. 2. Heat the oil in a large skillet over medium-high heat. Working in batches, brown moose (or beef) cubes; add to slow cooker. 3. Add the onion, jalapeño, celery, and garlic to the skillet; sauté for 3 minutes, then add to slow cooker. 4. Pour the water or broth and remaining ingredients except the wild rice, salt, and pepper into the slow cooker. Cover and cook on low for 4–6 hours or until meat is tender. 5. When finished, stir in the rice; add salt and pepper.

Fresh Minestrone Soup

Prep Time: 10 minutes | Cook Time: 4-6 hours | Serves: 8

3 cloves garlic, minced
1 (15-ounce) can fire-roasted diced tomatoes
1 (28-ounce) can crushed tomatoes
2 stalks celery, diced
1 medium onion, diced
3 medium carrots, diced
3 cups homemade or store-bought vegetable broth
2 (15-ounce) cans kidney beans, drained and rinsed
2 tablespoons tomato paste

2 tablespoons minced basil
2 tablespoons minced oregano
2 tablespoons minced Italian parsley
1½ cups shredded cabbage
¾ cup diced zucchini
1 teaspoon salt
½ teaspoon pepper
8 ounces small cooked pasta

1. In a 4-quart slow cooker, add the garlic, diced and crushed tomatoes, celery, onion, carrots, broth, beans, tomato paste, basil, and spices. Cover and cook on low heat for 6–8 hours. 2. Add the shredded cabbage and zucchini and turn to high for the last hour. 3. When finished, stir in the salt, pepper, and pasta before serving.

Tasty Italian Wedding Soup

Prep Time: 10 minutes | Cook Time: 4 hours | Serves: 4

1 pound frozen meatballs, thawed
6 cups chicken stock
1 pound escarole or baby spinach, coarsely chopped

2 large eggs
Salt and freshly ground black pepper, to taste

1. Add the meatballs, broth, and escarole (reserve spinach, if using) to the slow cooker; cover and cook on low for 4 hours. 2. Remove the meatballs to a serving bowl with a slotted spoon and cover to keep warm. Increase the setting of the slow cooker to high. Add spinach now if using. Cook uncovered while preparing next step. 3. Add the salt, eggs, and pepper to a small bowl; whisk to blend. 4. Stir the soup in the slow cooker in a circular motion, and then drizzle the egg mixture into the moving broth. Use a fork to separate the eggs into thin strands. Once the eggs are set, pour soup over the meatballs.

Homemade Tortilla Soup

Prep Time: 10 minutes | Cook Time: 4 hours | Serves: 8

2 tablespoons olive oil
1 large onion, chopped
2 cloves garlic, minced
2 tablespoons soy sauce
7 cups homemade or store-bought vegetable broth
12 ounces firm silken tofu, crumbled
2 cups tomato, diced
1 cup corn kernels

1 teaspoon chipotle powder
1 teaspoon cayenne pepper
2 teaspoons ground cumin
2 teaspoons salt
1 teaspoon dried oregano
10 small corn tortillas, sliced
8 ounces shredded Monterey jack cheese or vegan cheese, such as Daiya Mozzarella Style Shreds

1. In a sauté pan over medium heat, add the olive oil; sauté the onion until just soft, about 3 minutes. Add the garlic and sauté for an additional 30 seconds. 2. In a 4-quart slow cooker, pour all ingredients except tortillas and cheese. Stir, cover, and cook on low heat for 4 hours.
While cooking the soup, preheat oven to 450°F. Slice the corn tortillas into thin strips and place them on an ungreased baking sheet. Bake for about 10 minutes, or until they turn golden brown. Remove from heat and set aside. 3. After the soup has cooled slightly, use an immersion blender or regular blender to purée the soup. 4. Serve with cooked tortilla strips and 1 ounce of shredded cheese in each bowl of soup.

Broccoli Soup

Prep Time: 15 minutes | Cook Time: 3 to 4 hours | Serves: 6

2 medium heads broccoli
½ medium onion, diced
1 tablespoon extra-virgin olive oil
1 tablespoon ground turmeric
½ teaspoon garlic powder

½ teaspoon ground ginger
1 teaspoon freshly squeezed lemon juice
½ teaspoon sea salt
4 cups vegetable broth
Freshly ground black pepper

1. In your slow cooker, mix together the broccoli, olive oil, onion, turmeric, ginger, garlic powder, salt, lemon juice, and broth, and season with pepper. 2. Cover and cook on low for 3 to 4 hours and serve.

Cilantro Black Bean Soup

Prep Time: 10 minutes | Cook Time: 4 hours | Serves: 6

2 tablespoons olive oil
2 cloves garlic, minced
1 green bell pepper, diced, divided
1 red bell pepper, diced, divided
1 red onion, diced, divided
2 (15-ounce) cans black beans, drained and rinsed

2 teaspoons cumin, minced
1 teaspoon chipotle powder
4 cups homemade or store-bought vegetable broth
1 teaspoon kosher salt, or to taste
Frank's RedHot Sauce (optional, to taste)
¼ cup packed cilantro leaves and stems, chopped

1. In a sauté pan, heat the olive oil over medium heat, then sauté the garlic along with half each of the bell peppers and onion for 2–3 minutes. 2. In a 4-quart slow cooker, add the sautéed vegetables, black beans, cumin, chipotle powder, and broth. Cover, and cook on low for 6 hours. 3. Using an immersion blender, process the soup so that most of the soup is smooth. Add the salt to taste, adding more salt as necessary. Optionally, add a few drops of Frank's RedHot Sauce. 4. Ladle out the soup into bowls. Sprinkle each serving evenly with the cilantro and the remaining onion and peppers.

Low-Carb Turkey Slaw Soup

Prep Time: 5 minutes | Cook Time: 6-8 hours | Serves: 6

1 pound 93% lean ground turkey
1 (12-ounce) package broccoli slaw
4 cups Chicken Stock
1 (15-ounce) can low-sodium or no-salt-added diced tomatoes
1 small onion, diced

2 garlic cloves, minced
1 tablespoon Italian seasoning
1 teaspoon salt
½ teaspoon freshly ground black pepper
Handful chopped fresh parsley for garnish (optional)

1. Add the turkey, broccoli slaw, stock, tomatoes, garlic, Italian seasoning, salt, onion, and pepper to a slow cooker. Stir to mix well. 2. Cook on low for 6 to 8 hours or on high for 3 to 4 hours. Garnish with the parsley, if using.

Aromatic Kofta Soup

Prep Time: 15 minutes | Cook Time: 6-8 hours | Serves: 4

1 pound 93% lean ground beef
1 small onion, diced
2 garlic cloves, minced
1 tablespoon parsley
2 teaspoons coriander
1 teaspoon cumin
½ teaspoon salt
½ teaspoon freshly ground black pepper

¼ teaspoon nutmeg
¼ teaspoon mint
¼ teaspoon paprika
5 cups low-sodium beef broth
1 cup cauliflower florets
2 carrots, diced
2 tablespoons tomato paste

1. In a large bowl, mix together the beef, onion, salt, garlic, parsley, coriander, cumin, pepper, nutmeg, mint, and paprika until well blended. 2. Using your hands, form meatballs about 1 inch in diameter, and place them on a large plate. 3. In a slow cooker, combine together the broth, cauliflower, carrots, and tomato paste. 4. Add the meatballs and cook on low for 6 to 8 hours or on high for 3 to 4 hours. 5. When finished, serve.

Nutritious Egg Roll Soup

Prep Time: 10 minutes | Cook Time: 6-8 hours | Serves: 4

1 pound 93% lean ground beef
5 cups low-sodium beef, chicken, or vegetable broth
1 small onion, diced
1 (12-ounce) package broccoli slaw
8 ounces green cabbage, shredded
1 teaspoon sesame oil (regular or toasted)
2 scallions (whites and greens), sliced

¼ cup low-sodium soy sauce or coconut aminos
¼ cup rice wine vinegar
½ teaspoon salt
¼ teaspoon freshly ground black pepper
3 garlic cloves, minced
1 tablespoon minced fresh ginger

1. Add the beef, broth, onion, slaw, cabbage, sesame oil, scallions, vinegar, salt, soy sauce, pepper, garlic, and ginger to a slow cooker. 2. Cook on low for 6 to 8 hours or on high for 3 to 4 hours. 3. When finished, serve.

Low-Carb Cabbage Roll Soup

Prep Time: 5 minutes | Cook Time: 6-8 hours | Serves: 6

2 cups chopped cabbage
1 pound 93% lean ground beef
2 cups riced cauliflower
1 (28-ounce) can low-sodium or no-salt-added diced tomatoes
½ cup low-sodium beef broth

1 small onion, diced
3 garlic cloves, minced
1 tablespoon Italian seasoning
½ teaspoon salt
½ teaspoon freshly ground black pepper

1.Add the cabbage, beef, cauliflower, tomatoes, broth, garlic, Italian seasoning, salt, onion, and pepper to a slow cooker. Stir to mix well. 2.Cook on low for 6 to 8 hours or on high for 3 to 4 hours.
Make it faster: Add the ingredients to an Instant Pot and cook on Manual for 10 minutes. Release the pressure naturally.

Kale & Beans Chili

Prep Time: 15 minutes | Cook Time: 6 to 8 hours | Serves: 6

2 cups dried cannellini beans, soaked in water overnight, drained, and rinsed well
1 small bunch kale, washed, chopped, and de-ribbed
1 small onion, diced
½ green bell pepper, seeded and chopped
1 (4-ounce) can Hatch green chiles

4 cups vegetable broth
½ teaspoon garlic powder
1 teaspoon chili powder
½ teaspoon ground cumin
2 tablespoons extra-virgin olive oil
1 avocado, peeled, pitted, and chopped

1. In your slow cooker, mix together the beans, kale, chiles, onion, bell pepper, broth, chili powder, garlic powder, and cumin. 2. Cover and cook on low for 6 to 8 hours. 3. Once done, divide the food among serving bowls and drizzle each bowl with the olive oil. Top with avocado and serve.

Coconut Pork Stew with Pumpkin & Peanuts

Prep Time: 20 minutes | Cook Time: 8 hours | Serves: 8

2 tablespoons coconut oil
1½ pounds boneless pork ribs
Kosher salt
Freshly ground black pepper
½ onion, chopped
1 garlic clove, minced
1 jalapeño pepper, seeded and minced
1 teaspoon minced fresh ginger

1½ cups chicken broth
3 cups canned coconut milk
1 cup pumpkin purée
¼ cup all-natural peanut butter
¼ cup erythritol
1 teaspoon freshly squeezed lime juice
¼ cup chopped fresh cilantro
½ cup chopped toasted peanuts

1. In a large skillet, heat the coconut oil over medium-high heat. 2. Generously season the pork with the pepper and salt and add to the skillet. Cook for about 6 minutes until browned on both sides. Transfer to the slow cooker. 3. Return the skillet to medium-high heat and place in the onion, garlic, jalapeño, and ginger. Sauté until the onions are softened, about 3 minutes. 4. Stir in the chicken broth and bring to a boil. Cook for 1 minute. 5. Stir in the coconut milk, pumpkin, peanut butter, and erythritol until smooth. Pour the mixture into the slow cooker. Cover and cook for 8 hours on low. 6. Remove the meat from the slow cooker and cut it into bite-size pieces or shred it using two forks. Return the meat to the cooker. 7. Stir in the lime juice. Serve hot, garnished with the cilantro and peanuts.

Beef-Beans Chili

Prep Time: 20 minutes | Cook Time: 8 to 10 hours | Serves: 8

2 cups dry beans, rinsed and drained
2½ pounds sirloin tip, cut into 2-inch cubes
2 onions, chopped
6 garlic cloves, minced
2 jalapeño peppers, minced

4 large tomatoes, seeded and chopped
11 cups roasted vegetable broth
1 (6-ounce) BPA-free can tomato paste
2 tablespoons chili powder
1 teaspoon ground cumin

1. Combine all of the ingredients in your slow cooker. 2. Cover and cook on low for 8 to 10 hours until the beans are tender. Serve warm.

Sausage, Beans & Kale Soup

Prep Time: 15 minutes | Cook Time: 6 to 7 hours | Serves: 6

1-pound pre-cooked pork sausage, thinly sliced into coins
2 (15-ounce) cans cannellini beans, rinsed and drained well
5 carrots, diced
1 medium onion, diced
1 celery stalk, minced
2 bay leaves

1 teaspoon garlic powder
½ teaspoon dried oregano
½ teaspoon dried basil leaves
6 cups broth of choice
4 cups shredded, de-ribbed kale

1. Combine the sausage, carrots, beans, celery, onion, bay leaves, garlic powder, basil, oregano, broth, and kale in your slow cooker. 2. Cover and cook on low for 6 to 7 hours. 3. Remove and discard the bay leaves before serving.

Turmeric Lentil Soup

Prep Time: 15 minutes | Cook Time: 6 to 8 hours | Serves: 6

1 cup dried yellow lentils, soaked in water overnight, drained, and rinsed well
4 cups vegetable broth
1 small onion, diced
1 carrot, diced
1 celery stalk, minced
2 teaspoons ground turmeric

1 teaspoon garlic powder
½ teaspoon sea salt
½ teaspoon ground ginger
½ teaspoon ground cumin
½ teaspoon dried thyme leaves
¼ teaspoon ground cinnamon
2 cups full-fat coconut milk

1. In a slow cooker, mix together the lentils, onion, celery, carrot, broth, turmeric, ginger, garlic, thyme, salt, cumin, and cinnamon. 2. Cover and cook on low for 6 to 8 hours. 3. Stir in the coconut milk and serve.

Caramelized Onion and Beet Soup

Prep Time: 20 minutes | Cook Time: 6¼ to 7¼ hours | Serves: 8

8 large beets, peeled and cubed
2 cups caramelized onions and garlic
3 large carrots, peeled and chopped
8 cups roasted vegetable broth
5 tablespoons tomato paste

1 bay leaf
1 teaspoon dried dill weed
1 cup sour cream
2 tablespoons cornstarch

1. Combine the beets, carrots, onions, tomato paste, bay leaf, vegetable broth, and dill weed in your slow cooker. Cover and cook on low for 6 to 7 hours, until the beets and carrots are soft. 2. Remove and discard the bay leaf. 3. Using an immersion blender, mash some of the vegetables right in the slow cooker if desired. 4. Mix the sour cream, cornstarch and some of the liquid from the hot soup until well combined and stir into the soup. 5. Cover and cook on low for an additional 15 to 20 minutes, or until the soup thickens.

Pork & Sweet Potato Chowder

Prep Time: 20 minutes | Cook Time: 6¼ to 8¼ hours | Serves: 8

1 (3-pound) pork loin, cut into 1½-inch cubes
2 leeks, chopped
4 large sweet potatoes, peeled and cubed
2 cups frozen corn
4 garlic cloves, minced

3 tablespoons grated fresh ginger root
1 teaspoon ground ginger
8 cups roasted vegetable broth
⅔ cup 2% milk
2 tablespoons cornstarch

1. Combine the pork, sweet potatoes, corn, leeks, garlic, ground ginger, ginger root, and vegetable broth in your slow cooker. Cover and cook on low for 6 to 8 hours until the sweet potatoes are tender. 2. Whisk the milk and cornstarch in a small bowl until well blended. Stir this mixture into the slow cooker. 3. Cover and cook on low for 15 to 20 minutes more, or until the chowder is thickened.

Three Beans Chili

Prep Time: 15 minutes | Cook Time: 7 to 8 hours | Serves: 10

1 large yellow onion, chopped
2 cups chopped celery, chopped
1 yellow bell pepper, cored and chopped
1 orange bell pepper, cored and chopped
1 red bell pepper, cored and chopped
½ teaspoon sea salt, plus more for seasoning
4 (28-ounce) cans crushed tomatoes
2 (15-ounce) cans kidney beans, drained and rinsed
1 (15-ounce) can cannellini beans, drained and rinsed
1 (15-ounce) can black beans, drained and rinsed
4 teaspoons minced garlic

2 to 3 teaspoons chili powder (more if you want it spicier)
3 to 4 tablespoons ground cumin
2 teaspoons dried oregano
Ground black pepper
Sliced avocado, chopped fresh cilantro, or sliced scallions, for topping (optional)
1 to 1¼ cups shredded Cheddar or Monterey Jack cheese, for topping (optional)
1 to 1¼ cups guacamole, for topping (optional)
1 to 1¼ cups sour cream, for topping (optional)

1. Grease the bottom of the slow cooker with olive oil. 2. Set the heat to high. Add the onion, bell peppers, celery, and salt. Cook, stirring frequently, for 3 to 4 minutes, until the vegetables start to sizzle. 3. Reduce the heat to low. Add the kidney beans, cannellini beans, tomatoes, black beans, garlic, cumin, chili powder, and oregano. Season with salt and pepper. Cover and cook on low for 7 to 8 hours, or until the vegetables are soft and the beans are easily mashed. 4. Before serving, top with any combination of avocado, cilantro, or scallions (if using); 2 tablespoons of cheese per serving (if using); 2 tablespoons of guacamole per serving (if using); or 2 tablespoons of sour cream per serving (if using). Sprinkle with the cilantro or scallions and serve the chili warm. 5. Refrigerate leftovers for up to 1 week, or freeze for up to 3 months.

Curried Sirloin and Sweet Potato Stew

Prep Time: 20 minutes | Cook Time: 7 to 9 hours | Serves: 8

2 pounds sirloin tip, cut into 2-inch pieces
2 onions, chopped
3 garlic cloves, minced
2 large sweet potatoes, peeled and cubed
⅔ cup chopped dried apricots

⅔ cup golden raisins
5 large tomatoes, seeded and chopped
9 cups beef stock
2 teaspoons curry powder
1 cup whole-wheat couscous, cooked according to package directions

1. In your slow cooker, combine the sirloin, onions, sweet potatoes, garlic, apricots, tomatoes, raisins, beef stock, and curry powder. Cover and cook on low for 7 to 9 hours until the sweet potatoes are tender. 2. Stir in the couscous. Cover and let rest for 5 to 10 minutes, or until the couscous has softened. 3. Stir the stew and serve.

Savory Vegetable Curry

Prep Time: 20 minutes | Cook Time: 6 to 8 hours | Serves: 8

2 onions, chopped
3 garlic cloves, minced
2 medium zucchini, cut into 1-inch slices
2 medium sweet potatoes, peeled and cut into chunks
3 cups broccoli florets
4 large carrots, peeled and cut into chunks

1 (8 ounce) package button mushrooms, sliced
2 red bell peppers, stemmed, seeded, and chopped
5 cups roasted vegetable broth
1 cup canned coconut milk
2 to 4 tablespoons yellow curry paste

1. In your slow cooker, combine all the ingredients. Cover and cook on low for 6 to 8 hours until the vegetables are tender. 2. Serve in soup bowls over hot cooked brown rice, if desired.

Thai Chicken Tom Yum Soup

Prep Time: 5 minutes | Cook Time: 5 hours | Serves: 4

10 oz boneless, skinless chicken breasts, sliced
7 oz mushrooms, sliced
2-3 tomatoes, sliced

4 cups water
2 tbsp tom yum paste

1. Add water, tom yum paste and chicken breasts to the slow cooker and stir to mix well. 2. Close the lid and cook on low for 4 hours. 3. Then add mushrooms and tomatoes. Stir and close the lid. Cook for one hour longer.

Cheesy Chicken Soup

Prep Time: 5 minutes | Cook Time: 8 hours | Serves: 4

1½ lb skinless, boneless, chicken pieces
2 cups chicken broth

8 oz Pepper Jack cheese, cubed
15 oz chunky salsa

1. Place the chicken pieces on the bottom of the slow cooker. 2. Add remaining ingredients and stir until well combined. 3. Cover and cook on low for 8 hours. 4. Remove chicken pieces and shred, return to the pot. Stir gently. 5. Serve hot.

Tomato-Nuts Soup

Prep Time: 5 minutes | Cook Time: 6-8 hours | Serves: 6

7 large ripe tomatoes
½ cup raw macadamia nuts
4 cups water or vegetable broth

1 medium onion, chopped
Seasoning: salt, pepper, basil to taste

1. In a nonstick skillet over medium heat, brown the onions for 5 minutes. 2. Add all ingredients to the slow cooker and stir to mix well. Cook on low for 6-8 hours. 3. Purée until smooth with a blender. Serve warm.

Beef, Tomato and Sweet Potato Stew

Prep Time: 15 minutes | Cook Time: 6 to 8 hours | Serves: 4

2 pounds extra-lean ground beef
1 pound sweet potatoes, peeled and chopped, or red potatoes, chopped
1 (28-ounce) can diced tomatoes, with their juice
1 (15-ounce) can diced tomatoes, with their juice
1 onion, chopped
1 red or green bell pepper, seeded and chopped

2 celery stalks, chopped
2 garlic cloves, minced
Handful chopped fresh parsley
1½ teaspoons ground mustard
1 teaspoon garlic powder
1 teaspoon salt
½ teaspoon freshly ground black pepper

1. Combine all the ingredients in the slow cooker and stir to mix well. 2. Cover and cook on low for 6 to 8 hours. Serve warm.

Lentil Tomato Stew

Prep Time: 10 minutes | Cook Time: 6 to 8 hours | Serves: 4

2 pounds Roma tomatoes, diced
1 cup lentils, rinsed and drained
1 (32-ounce) carton low-sodium vegetable broth
¼ cup chopped fresh basil

1 tablespoon balsamic vinegar
4 garlic cloves, minced
1 teaspoon salt
½ teaspoon freshly ground black pepper

1. Combine all the ingredients in the slow cooker and stir to mix well. 2. Cover and cook on low for 6 to 8 hours until the lentils are tender. Serve warm.

Beef & Sweet Potato Stew

Prep Time: 10 minutes | Cook Time: 8 to 9 hours | Serves: 4

2 pounds beef stew meat
1 pound sweet potatoes, peeled and chopped
3 medium carrots, peeled and chopped
1 medium onion, chopped

2 celery stalks, chopped
1 teaspoon salt
½ teaspoon freshly ground black pepper
1 (32-ounce) carton low-sodium beef broth

1. Combine the meat, onion, sweet potatoes, celery, carrots, salt, and pepper in the slow cooker. 2. Pour in the broth. 3. Cover and cook on low for 8 to 9 hours.

Spicy Sweet Potato & Chickpeas Curry

Prep Time: 15 minutes | Cook Time: 6 to 8 hours | Serves: 4

1 pound sweet potatoes, peeled and chopped
1 onion, chopped
2 carrots, peeled and chopped
1 (15-ounce) can chickpeas, rinsed and drained
1 (15-ounce) can light coconut milk
1 cup water
1 cup frozen green peas
4 garlic cloves, minced

2 Roma tomatoes, chopped, plus extra for garnish
2 teaspoons ground cumin
1 teaspoon ground ginger
1 teaspoon ground turmeric
1 teaspoon dried thyme
1 teaspoon salt
1 teaspoon cayenne pepper
Chopped fresh cilantro, for garnish

1. Combine all the ingredients in the slow cooker and stir to mix well. 2. Cover and cook on low for 6 to 8 hours. 3. Garnish with chopped tomatoes and cilantro. Serve warm.

Savory Beef and Barley Soup

Prep Time: 15 minutes | Cook Time: 8 hours | Serves: 8

3 cups chicken broth
3 cups beef broth
1 tablespoon tomato paste
2 cups frozen mirepoix
1½ pounds beef chuck roast, trimmed of excess fat and cut into bite-size pieces
⅔ cup pearl barley (not quick-cooking)

8 ounces sliced mushrooms
1 bay leaf
1 teaspoon onion powder
1 teaspoon garlic powder
¾ teaspoon dried thyme
1 teaspoon salt, plus more for seasoning
½ teaspoon freshly ground black pepper, plus more for seasoning

1. Combine all the ingredients in the slow cooker and stir to mix well. 2. Cover and cook on low for 8 hours. 3. Discard the bay leaf. Season with more salt and pepper if needed. Ladle into bowls and serve warm.

Parmesan Tomato Soup

Prep Time: 10 minutes | Cook Time: 8 hours | Serves: 6

1 cup frozen mirepoix
⅓ cup all-purpose flour
1 (28-ounce) can crushed tomatoes
1 (6-ounce) can tomato paste
1 tablespoon dried basil
1 teaspoon dried oregano
1 teaspoon salt, plus more for seasoning

4 cups chicken or vegetable broth
1 bay leaf
1 cup milk, warmed
2 tablespoons unsalted butter
Freshly ground black pepper
⅔ cup grated Parmesan cheese

1. Combine the flour, mirepoix, crushed tomatoes, tomato paste, oregano, basil, and salt in the slow cooker. Whisk until they are well incorporate. Pour in the broth. Add the bay leaf. 2. Cover with the lid and cook on low for 8 hours. 3. Discard the bay leaf. Add the warm milk and butter; stir until the butter is melted. Season with more salt and pepper, if desired. 4. Ladle the soup into serving bowls, top each serving with Parmesan cheese, and serve.

Black Bean Ham Soup

Prep Time: 10 minutes | Cook Time: 8 hours | Serves: 6

8 ounces dried black beans, picked over and rinsed
3½ cups water
1 smoked ham hock, rinsed
1 bay leaf
1 teaspoon dried oregano
1 teaspoon ground cumin

1 teaspoon garlic powder
1 teaspoon salt, plus more for seasoning
Juice of 1 lime
1 (8-ounce) can tomato sauce
Freshly ground black pepper
Chopped fresh cilantro, for garnish

1. Combine the black beans, ham hock, water, bay leaf, cumin, oregano, garlic powder, and salt in the slow cooker. 2. Cover with the lid and cook on low for 8 hours, or until the beans are tender. 3. Discard the bay leaf. Stir in the lime juice and tomato sauce. Season with additional salt and pepper, if desired. 4. Ladle into soup bowls and garnish with cilantro. Serve warm.

French Onion Bread Soup

Prep Time: 15 minutes | Cook Time: 8 hours | Serves: 4

3 small yellow onions, cut into thin rings
¼ cup olive oil or canola oil
Pinch salt
Pinch freshly ground black pepper
Pinch sugar

2 (13.5-ounce) cans beef consommé
½ cup water
4 slices crusty bread (French bread or a baguette works well)
1⅓ cups shredded Gruyère cheese

1. Place the onions in the slow cooker. Add the salt, olive oil, black pepper, and sugar and todd until the onions are well coated. 2. Cover and cook on low for 8 hours until the onions are soft and caramelized. 3. Pour in the consommé and water and turn the heat to high. Cook for about 10 minutes. 4. Ladle soup into four oven-safe bowls and place on a rimmed baking sheet. Top each serving of soup with a piece of bread. Sprinkle each piece of bread with ⅓ cup Gruyère cheese. 5. Bake in your air fryer for 1 to 2 minutes, until cheese is melted and beginning to brown. Serve immediately.

Lemony Lentil Chicken Soup

Prep Time: 15 minutes | Cook Time: 6 hours | Serves: 6

1 medium yellow onion, very thinly sliced
1 cup brown lentils
1 pound boneless, skinless chicken thighs, trimmed of excess fat
1 teaspoon garlic powder
5 cups chicken broth

3 large egg yolks
¼ cup fresh lemon juice
Salt
Freshly ground black pepper

1. In the slow cooker, combine the chicken, onion, lentils, garlic powder, and chicken broth. 2. Cover with the lid and cook on low for 6 hours. 3. Transfer the chicken to a cutting board and shred the chicken with two forks. Then return it to the slow cooker. 4. Whisk together the egg yolks and lemon juice in a small bowl. Stir the mixture into the slow cooker. Season with salt and black pepper. Serve.

Summer Vegetable Soup

Prep Time: 10 minutes | Cook Time: 7 to 8 hours | Serves: 8

4 medium potatoes such as Yukon gold, cut into 1-inch cubes
2 cups peeled and cubed butternut squash (about 1½ pounds)
2 small yellow squash or zucchini, sliced
4 celery stalks, chopped
3 large carrots, chopped
1 medium onion, chopped
4 garlic cloves, peeled
¼ cup packed fresh cilantro

¼ cup packed fresh basil leaves
2 tablespoons extra-virgin olive oil
6 cups savory vegetable broth or low-sodium vegetable broth
⅛ teaspoon salt
Freshly ground black pepper
4 cups baby spinach
Juice of ½ lemon

1. Place the potatoes, yellow squash, butternut squash, celery, and carrots in the slow cooker. 2. Add the onion, cilantro, basil, garlic, and olive oil to a food processor. Blend until it achieves a chunky consistency. Pour this mixture into the slow cooker. 3. Pour in the broth; sprinkle with salt, and pepper and stir to mix well. Cover and cook on low heat for 7 to 8 hours. 4. Stir in the spinach and lemon juice about 30 minutes before serving. 5. Serve warm.

Homemade Chicken Tortilla Soup

Prep Time: 15 minutes | Cook Time: 7 to 8 hours | Serves: 6

1½ pounds boneless, skinless chicken breasts
6 cups chicken stock or low-sodium chicken broth
1 (14.5-ounce) can black beans, drained and rinsed
1 (14.5-ounce) can whole kernel corn, drained and rinsed
1 (14.5-ounce) can no-salt-added diced fire-roasted tomatoes
3 garlic cloves, minced
1 medium onion, finely chopped

2 bell peppers (any color), chopped
1 tablespoon chili powder
2 teaspoons ground cumin
¾ teaspoon smoked paprika
¼ cup freshly squeezed lime juice
Optional toppings: tortilla strips or chips, diced or sliced avocado, diced fresh tomatoes, shredded cheese, chopped cilantro, or sour cream

1. Place the chicken, stock, corn, tomatoes, black beans, garlic, bell peppers, onion, cumin, chili powder, and paprika in the slow cooker and stir to mix well. Cover and cook on low for 7 to 8 hours, or until chicken is tender and cooked through. 2. Remove chicken and shred it with two forks. Return chicken to the slow cooker and stir in the lime juice. Cook until the chicken is heated through again. 3. Serve warm with toppings to your liking.

Squash and Red Lentil Stew

Prep Time: 10 minutes | Cook Time: 7 to 8 hours | Serves: 6

6 cups savory vegetable broth or low-sodium vegetable broth
3 pounds kabocha squash or butternut squash, peeled, seeded, and cut into 1-inch cubes (about 4 to 4½ cups)
1 (28-ounce) can no-salt-added diced tomatoes
1 cup red lentils
2 large carrots, cut into ½-inch pieces

1 large onion, chopped
1 jalapeño pepper, seeded and minced
3 garlic cloves, minced
1 tablespoon garam masala
Freshly ground black pepper

1. Combine the squash, broth, tomatoes, carrots, lentils, onion, jalapeño, garam masala, garlic, and pepper in your slow cooker. Cover and cook on low for 7 to 8 hours. 2. Garnish with the cilantro and serve warm.

Lamb Chickpea Stew

Prep Time: 10 minutes | Cook Time: 7 to 8 hours | Serves: 8

2 pounds boneless lamb stew meat, cut into 1-inch chunks, or 2½ pounds lamb shoulder chops, deboned and trimmed
1 (28-ounce) can no-salt-added diced tomatoes
1 (14.5-ounce) can chickpeas, drained and rinsed
¾ cup beef stock or low-sodium beef broth
1 large onion, chopped
2 garlic cloves, minced

2 teaspoons grated fresh ginger
2 teaspoons ground cumin
½ teaspoon ground cinnamon
½ teaspoon dried mint
¼ teaspoon freshly ground black pepper
1 tablespoon freshly squeezed lemon juice
Pinch salt

1. Place the lamb in the slow cooker. Add the tomatoes, chickpeas, onion, garlic, stock, ginger, cumin, mint, cinnamon, and pepper and stir to mix well. Cover and cook on low for 7 to 8 hours. 2. Then stir in the lemon juice and salt. Let the stew rest for 5 minutes to allow the flavors to blend. Serve warm.

Chapter 7 Sauce, Dip and Dressings

Delicious Spicy Cheese Sauce or Dip

Prep Time: 5 minutes | Cook Time: 1 hour | Serves: 2¼ cups

1 cup shredded sharp Cheddar cheese
½ cup heavy (whipping) cream
½ cup cream cheese
¼ cup ghee or unsalted butter
½ teaspoon cayenne pepper

½ teaspoon garlic powder
½ teaspoon onion powder
½ teaspoon paprika
Pinch kosher salt

1. In the slow cooker, stir together all the ingredients. 2. Cover and cook for 30 to 60 minutes on low. Whisk, if needed, to combine. 3. Serve hot, or cool to room temperature and refrigerate for up to 1 week. Reheat in the top of a double boiler or in 30-second intervals on high in the microwave.

Rich Gorgonzola Cream Sauce

Prep Time: 5 minutes | Cook Time: 1 hour | Serves: 3 cups

2 cups heavy (whipping) cream
1⅓ cups Gorgonzola cheese

½ cup grated Parmesan cheese
½ teaspoon freshly ground black pepper

1. In the slow cooker, stir together all the ingredients. 2. Cover and cook for 30 to 60 minutes on low. Whisk, if needed, to combine. Serve hot.

Flavorful Sweet Blueberry Syrup

Prep Time: 5 minutes | Cook Time: 4 hours | Serves: 2½ cups

1 cup frozen blueberries
1 cup water
2 teaspoons freshly squeezed lemon juice

½ cup erythritol or ½ teaspoon stevia powder
¼ teaspoon xanthan gum
½ teaspoon pure vanilla extract (optional)

1. In the slow cooker, mix the blueberries, water, lemon juice, and erythritol. Cover and cook for 4 hours on low or 2 hours on low. Whisk to combine. 2. Transfer ½ cup of the syrup to a small bowl. Whisk in the xanthan gum until very well incorporated. Whisk the mixture back into the syrup in the slow cooker. 3. Whisk in the vanilla (if using). 4. Serve warm or chilled. Store the sauce in an airtight container in the refrigerator for up to 1 week or in the freezer for up to 3 months.

Rich Sweet Caramel Sauce

Prep Time: 5 minutes | Cook Time: 8 hours | Serves: 2 cups

1¼ cups heavy (whipping) cream
1 cup brown sugar erythritol blend (such as Sukrin Gold) or 1 cup erythritol plus 2 teaspoons blackstrap molasses
½ cup (1 stick) unsalted butter or ghee

Pinch fine sea salt
¼ teaspoon xanthan gum
½ teaspoon pure vanilla extract

1. In the slow cooker, combine the heavy cream, brown sugar erythritol blend, butter, and sea salt. Cover and cook for 8 hours on low. When finished, whisk the mixture to combine. 2. Transfer ½ cup of the sauce to a small bowl. Whisk in the xanthan gum until very well incorporated. Whisk the mixture back into the sauce in the slow cooker. 3. Whisk in the vanilla. 4. Transfer the sauce to a bowl or jar and let cool. It will thicken as it cools. 5. Serve warm. Refrigerate any leftovers for up to 1 week or freeze for up to 3 months. Reheat in 30-second intervals on high in the microwave.

Rich Dreamy Hot Chocolate Sauce

Prep Time: 5 minutes | Cook Time: 1 hour | Serves: 3 cups

2 cups heavy (whipping) cream
4 ounces unsweetened chocolate, finely chopped

⅔ cup erythritol
1 teaspoon pure vanilla extract

1. In the slow cooker, combine the heavy cream, chocolate, and erythritol. Cover and cook for 1 hour on low heat. When finished, stir to combine. 2. Whisk in the vanilla. Serve hot. 3. Refrigerate leftovers for up to 1 week. Reheat the sauce in the slow cooker, in the top of a double boiler, or in the microwave in 30-second intervals on high.

Classic Marinara Sauce

Prep Time: 5 minutes | Cook Time: 12 hours | Serves: 8

1 tablespoon olive oil
1 large onion, diced
2 cloves garlic, minced
1 tablespoon minced fresh basil
1 tablespoon minced fresh Italian parsley

1 stalk celery, diced
1 (28-ounce) can whole tomatoes in purée
1 (28-ounce) can crushed tomatoes
1 (15-ounce) can diced tomatoes in juice

1. Warm the olive oil in a medium nonstick skillet. Sauté the onion and garlic for about 3 minutes until the onion is soft. 2. Add the onions and garlic to a 6-quart slow cooker. Add the herbs, celery, and tomatoes. Stir to distribute the spices. Cook on low for 10–12 hours. 3. When finished, serve.

Traditional Chipotle Tomato Sauce

Prep Time: 5 minutes | Cook Time: 10 hours | Serves: 6

3 cloves garlic, minced
1 onion, minced
1 (28-ounce) can crushed tomatoes
1 (14-ounce) can diced tomatoes, undrained

3 chipotle peppers in adobo sauce, minced
1 teaspoon dried oregano
1 tablespoon minced cilantro
½ teaspoon freshly ground black pepper

1. Place all ingredients into a 4-quart slow cooker. Cook on low for 8–10 hours. 2. Stir before serving.

Easy Bean Dip

Prep Time: 5 minutes | Cook Time: 1 hour 30 minutes | Serves: 12

2 (15-ounce) cans pinto beans, drained and rinsed
1½ cups water
1 tablespoon olive oil
1 small onion, peeled and diced
3 cloves garlic, minced
1 medium tomato, seeded and diced

1 teaspoon chipotle powder
½ teaspoon ground cumin
¼ cup packed fresh cilantro leaves and stems, finely chopped
1 teaspoon kosher salt, plus more to taste
1 cup grated Monterey jack or Cheddar cheese

1. In a 4-quart slow cooker, add the beans, water, olive oil, onion, and garlic. Cover and cook over low heat for 1 hour. 2. Using a potato masher, partly mash the bean mixture. Let about half remain chunky. 3. Uncover the slow cooker and stir in diced tomato, chipotle, cumin, cilantro, and kosher salt. Re-cover and cook for another 30 minutes. Taste and add more salt if needed. 4. Scoop out dip into a serving bowl. Top with grated cheese; let sit for 5 minutes for cheese to partially melt, then serve immediately.

Classic Apple Butter

Prep Time: 5 minutes | Cook Time: 10 hours | Serves: 3 cups

4 pounds Jonathan, McIntosh, or Rome apples
1 lemon
1⅓ cups light brown sugar, packed

1 cup apple cider
6" cinnamon stick (optional)

1. Core and quarter the apples. Add to a 4- or 5-quart slow cooker. 2. Zest the lemon and squeeze out the juice into a small bowl. 3. Add the lemon zest, lemon juice, brown sugar, and cider to the slow cooker and stir to combine. Add the cinnamon stick if using. Cover and cook on low for 10 hours or until the apples are soft and tender. 4. Uncover and, stirring occasionally, cook on high for an additional 8–10 hours or until the mixture has reduced to about 3 cups. 5. If used, remove and discard the cinnamon stick. Use a spatula to press the apple butter through a large mesh strainer to remove the peel. Ladle the warm apple butter into hot, sterilized jars. Screw two-piece lids onto the jars. Allow to rest at room temperature for 8 hours; refrigerate for up to 6 months.

Simple Eggplant Caviar

Prep Time: 10 minutes | Cook Time: 8 hours | Serves: 8

2 medium-sized eggplants, peeled and cut across into ½" slices
½ cup plus 2 teaspoons kosher salt, divided
Cooking spray
¼ cup olive oil
1 small onion, peeled and diced

4 garlic cloves, minced
1 teaspoon ground black pepper
1 tablespoon red wine vinegar
1 loaf Italian bread, cut into ¼" slices and toasted

1. Add the eggplant slices in a colander in the sink. Use the ½ cup of the kosher salt to evenly salt both sides of eggplant slices. Let sit for 30 minutes, then rinse the slices and pat dry with paper towels. Cut into 1" chunks. 2. Spray the insides of a 4-quart slow cooker with the cooking spray. Add in the eggplant chunks. Stir in the olive oil, onion, garlic, remaining 2 teaspoons salt, and the pepper. Cover and cook on low for 6–8 hours, or until eggplant is very tender. 3. Mash eggplant mixture with a fork. Mix in red wine vinegar. Transfer to a serving bowl. Serve warm or chilled with toasted slices of Italian bread.

Yummy Creamy Hot Fudge Sauce

Prep Time: 10 minutes | Cook Time: 2 hours | Serves: 2 cups

1 (12-ounce) can evaporated milk
10 ounces semisweet or bittersweet chocolate chips
1 teaspoon vanilla extract

½ teaspoon unsalted butter
⅛ teaspoon table salt

1. Place all ingredients in a 1½- to 2-quart slow cooker. Cook on low heat, stirring occasionally, for 2 hours. The sauce will thicken as it cools. 2. Refrigerate leftovers. Reheat in the slow cooker for 1 hour on high or on the stovetop on low or simmer settings until warmed through, stirring frequently, about 10 minutes.

Healthy Spinach-Artichoke Dip

Prep Time: 10 minutes | Cook Time: 2 hours | Serves: 4

Cooking spray
1 tablespoon olive oil
2 cloves garlic, minced
1½ cups part-skim ricotta cheese
½ teaspoon thyme
1 teaspoon lemon zest

½ teaspoon cayenne pepper
1 (14-ounce) can artichoke hearts, drained and chopped
1 (10-ounce) package frozen spinach, thawed and drained well
¼ cup grated Parmesan cheese
½ teaspoon salt
¼ cup shredded mozzarella

1. Spray the inside of a 3- or 4-quart slow cooker with nonstick spray. 2. Heat the olive oil in a small nonstick skillet over medium heat. When hot, place in the garlic and cook until fragrant and pale golden, about 1 minute. Remove the skillet from the heat and let the garlic cool while proceeding with next step. 3. In a large mixing bowl, combine the thyme, lemon zest, ricotta cheese, and cayenne pepper. 4. Add the artichokes, spinach, Parmesan, salt, and cooled garlic. Stir well to combine. 5. Transfer the artichoke mixture into the prepared cooker and sprinkle evenly with the mozzarella. 6. Cover and cook on high for 2 hours. When finished, serve hot or warm.

Rich Fig and Ginger Spread

Prep Time: 5 minutes | Cook Time: 3 hours | Serves: 25

2 pounds fresh figs
2 tablespoons minced fresh ginger
2 tablespoons lime juice

½ cup water
¾ cup sugar

1. Place all ingredients in a 2-quart slow cooker. Stir. Cook on low for 2–3 hours. Remove the lid and cook for another 2–3 hours until the mixture is thickened. 2. Pour into airtight containers and refrigerate for up to 6 weeks.

Homemade Chimichurri Sauce

Prep Time: 5 minutes | Cook Time: 6 hours | Serves: 2 cups

2 cups fresh parsley leaves
1 cup extra-virgin olive oil
⅔ cup red wine vinegar
½ cup fresh cilantro

4 garlic cloves, peeled
1 teaspoon red pepper flakes
1 teaspoon ground cumin
½ teaspoon salt

1. Add the parsley, olive oil, vinegar, cilantro, garlic, red pepper flakes, cumin, and salt to the slow cooker. Stir to mix well. 2. Cook on low heat for 6 hours or on high heat for 3 hours. Let cool. 3. Transfer the cooled mixture to a food processor and pulse until a rough paste forms.

Tasty Cream of Mushroom Sauce

Prep Time: 10 minutes | Cook Time: 10 hours | Serves: 4 cups

1 pound mushrooms, chopped
3 cups Vegetable Broth or store-bought low-sodium vegetable broth
1 small onion, chopped
1 cup 2% reduced-fat milk
4 ounces low-fat cream cheese

¼ cup unsalted butter
1 garlic clove, minced
½ teaspoon salt
½ teaspoon freshly ground black pepper
¼ teaspoon thyme

1. Add the mushrooms, broth, onion, milk, cream cheese, butter, garlic, salt, pepper, and thyme to a slow cooker. Stir to mix well. 2. Cook on low for 8 to 10 hours or on high for 4 to 5 hours. 3. Once cooled, transfer the mixture to a food processor or a blender and process until smooth.

Super-Easy Ghee

Prep Time: 5 minutes | Cook Time: 6 hours | Serves: 4 cups

2 pounds unsalted butter

1. Add the butter to a slow cooker. Leave the lid slightly ajar to let steam escape. 2. Cook on low for 4 to 6 hours or on high for 2 to 3 hours. 3. Line a strainer with cheesecloth or a coffee filter, and set over a mason jar or a bowl. Carefully pour the liquid through the strainer and discard the solids. 4. Let the ghee cool. Store in a cool, dry place.

Low-Carb Ketchup

Prep Time: 5 minutes | Cook Time: 6 hours | Serves: 4 cups

2 cups low-sodium or no-salt-added tomato sauce
¼ cup apple cider vinegar
1 small onion, diced
2 garlic cloves, minced
1 tablespoon of powdered erythritol sweetener of your choice
1 tablespoon ground mustard

1 teaspoon salt
½ teaspoon Worcestershire sauce
¼ teaspoon freshly ground black pepper
¼ teaspoon cinnamon
¼ teaspoon paprika

1. Add the tomato sauce, vinegar, onion, garlic, erythritol, mustard, salt, Worcestershire sauce, pepper, cinnamon, and paprika to a slow cooker. Stir to mix well. 2. Cook on low for 4 to 6 hours or on high for 2 to 3 hours. 3. Once cooled, transfer the mixture to a blender and purée the sauce to your desired consistency.

Fresh Strawberry Sauce

Prep Time: 5 minutes | Cook Time: 6 hours | Serves: 1½ to 2 cups

2 cups diced fresh strawberries
1 teaspoon powdered erythritol sweetener of your choice

¼ teaspoon vanilla extract

1. Add the strawberries, erythritol, and vanilla to a slow cooker. Stir to mix well. 2. Cook on low for 4 to 6 hours or on high for 2 to 3 hours. 3. Transfer the mixture to a food processor or a blender and process until smooth.

Chapter 8 Desserts

Rick Hot Chocolate

Prep Time: 5 minutes | Cook Time: 1½ hours | Serves: 10-12

8 cups milk
1 (14-ounce) can sweetened condensed milk
2 cups semisweet chocolate chips

1½ teaspoons vanilla extract
1 teaspoon salt

1. Combine the milk, sweetened condensed milk, chocolate chips, vanilla, and salt in the slow cooker and stir. 2. Cover and cook on high heat for 1 hour. Whisk. If the chocolate is melted, it's ready to serve. If not, cover and cook for another 30 minutes and check again. 3. Turn the slow cooker to warm. Serve the hot chocolate in mugs.

Chewy Molasses-Pecan Wheat Berry Pudding

Prep Time: 5 minutes | Cook Time: 6-8 hours | Serves: 6

Nonstick cooking spray
1 cup wheat berries
1 ripe banana, mashed
1 tablespoon orange zest
1 teaspoon vanilla extract
1 teaspoon ground cinnamon

½ teaspoon ground nutmeg
1 (2-inch) piece ginger, minced
4 cups low-fat or nonfat milk, or plant-based milk
¼ cup molasses
½ cup chopped pecans

1. Spray the inside of a 6-quart slow cooker with the cooking spray. Add the wheat berries, banana, orange zest, vanilla, nutmeg, cinnamon, and ginger and stir to combine. 2. Pour in the milk and stir well to combine. Cover and cook on low heat for 6 to 8 hours. 3. When finished, stir in the molasses. Divide the pudding among 6 bowls and garnish with the pecans before serving.

Hearty Pumpkin Pie Oats

Prep Time: 5 minutes | Cook Time: 8-9 hours | Serves: 7

2 cups uncooked steel-cut oats
8 cups unsweetened almond milk
1 (15-ounce) can pumpkin purée
1½ tablespoons pumpkin pie spice

1½ teaspoons ground cinnamon
⅓ cup brown sugar
1 cup unsalted pecans, chopped

1. In a 4- to 6-quart slow cooker, combine the oats, almond milk, pumpkin pie spice, pumpkin purée, cinnamon, and brown sugar and mix well. 2. Cover with a lid and cook on low for 8 to 9 hours. When finished, stir well and serve warm, topped with pecans.

Basic Almond Golden Cake

Prep Time: 15 minutes | Cook Time: 3 hours | Serves: 8

½ cup coconut oil, divided
1½ cups almond flour
½ cup coconut flour
½ cup granulated erythritol
2 teaspoons baking powder

3 eggs
½ cup coconut milk
2 teaspoons pure vanilla extract
½ teaspoon almond extract

1. Line the insert of a 4-quart slow cooker with aluminum foil and grease the aluminum foil with 1 tablespoon of the coconut oil. 2. In a medium bowl, mix the coconut flour, erythritol, almond flour, and baking powder. 3. In a large bowl, whisk together the remaining coconut oil, eggs, coconut milk, vanilla, and almond extract. 4. Pour the dry ingredients into the wet ingredients and stir until well blended. 5. Transfer the batter to the insert and use a spatula to even the top. 6. Cover and cook on low for 3 hours, or until a toothpick inserted in the center comes out clean. 7. Remove the cake from the insert and cool completely before serving.

Yummy Peanut Butter Cup Cake

Prep Time: 15 minutes | Cook Time: 3-4 hours | Serves: 8

2 tablespoons coconut oil, divided
1 cup almond flour
1 cup granulated erythritol, divided
1 teaspoon baking powder
¼ teaspoon salt

¾ cup natural peanut butter
½ cup heavy (whipping) cream
1 teaspoon pure vanilla extract
1 cup boiling water
¼ cup cocoa powder

1. Lightly grease the insert of a 4-quart slow cooker with 1 tablespoon of the coconut oil. 2. In a large bowl, stir together the ½ cup of the erythritol, almond flour, baking powder, and salt. 3. In a medium bowl, whisk together the heavy cream, peanut butter, and vanilla until smooth. 4. Pour the peanut butter mixture into the dry ingredients and stir to combine. 5. Transfer the batter to the insert and spread it out evenly. 6. In a small bowl, stir together the remaining ½ cup of the erythritol, boiling water, and cocoa powder. 7. Pour the chocolate mixture over the batter. 8. Cover and cook on low for 3 to 4 hours. 9. Let the cake stand for 30 minutes and serve warm.

Winter Warm Gingerbread

Prep Time: 10 minutes | Cook Time: 3 hours | Serves: 8

1 tablespoon coconut oil
2 cups almond flour
¾ cup granulated erythritol
2 tablespoons coconut flour
2 tablespoons ground ginger
2 teaspoons baking powder
2 teaspoons ground cinnamon

½ teaspoon ground nutmeg
¼ teaspoon ground cloves
Pinch salt
¾ cup heavy (whipping) cream
½ cup butter, melted
4 eggs
1 teaspoon pure vanilla extract

1. Lightly grease the insert of the slow cooker with coconut oil. 2. In a large bowl, stir together the erythritol, coconut flour, almond flour, ginger, baking powder, cinnamon, nutmeg, cloves, and salt. 3. In a medium bowl, whisk together the heavy cream, butter, eggs, and vanilla. 4. Add the wet ingredients to the dry ingredients and stir to combine. 5. Spoon the batter into the insert. 6. Cover and cook on low for 3 hours, or until a toothpick inserted in the center comes out clean. 7. When finished, serve warm.

Holiday Chocolate-Covered Nut Clusters

Prep Time: 5 minutes | Cook Time: 2 hours | Serves: 18

1 (16-ounce) package chocolate or vanilla-flavored candy coating (almond bark)

1 (16-ounce) jar salted dry-roasted peanuts

1. Put the candy coating in the slow cooker. 2. Cover and cook on low heat for 1 hour. Stir. If needed, cook for another hour and stir again. 3. Stir the peanuts into the chocolate until coated. Use a spoon or a scoop to drop the peanut-chocolate mixture onto parchment paper. Allow to set completely for 1 hour before serving.

Tasty Toasted Almond Cheesecake

Prep Time: 15 minutes | Cook Time: 4 hours | Serves: 8

For the Crust:
1 cup toasted almonds, ground to a meal
1 large egg, lightly beaten
2 tablespoons coconut oil, melted
For the Filling:
2 large eggs
2 (8-ounce) packages cream cheese, at room temperature
¾ cup almond butter
¼ cup coconut cream

1 teaspoon stevia powder
1 cup water

1 teaspoon pure almond extract
¾ cup erythritol
1 tablespoon coconut flour
2 teaspoons stevia powder

1. To make the crust: mix the almond meal, egg, coconut oil, and stevia powder in a medium bowl. Press the mixture into the bottom of a baking pan that fits into your slow cooker (make sure there is room to lift the pan out). Many pans could work, depending on the size and shape of your slow cooker. 2. Pour the water into the slow cooker insert. Place the pan in the cooker. 3. To make the filling: beat the eggs, then beat in the cream cheese, almond butter, coconut cream, almond extract, erythritol, coconut flour, and stevia powder in a large bowl. Pour the mixture over the crust. Cover and cook for 4 hours on low or 2 hours on high. 4. When finished, turn off the slow cooker and let the cheesecake sit inside until cooled to room temperature, up to 3 hours. 5. Remove the pan from the slow cooker and refrigerate until chilled, about 2 hours more. Serve chilled.

Crispy Chocolate Chip Cookies

Prep Time: 10 minutes | Cook Time: 2½ hours | Serves: 10

¼ cup coconut oil, melted, plus more for coating the parchment
1 cup erythritol
1 teaspoon stevia powder
1 egg, beaten
½ teaspoon pure vanilla extract

1½ cups almond flour
1¾ teaspoons baking powder
½ teaspoon fine sea salt
4 ounces unsweetened chocolate, chopped
½ cup chopped toasted walnuts

1. Line a slow cooker insert with enough parchment or wax paper to extend over the sides slightly. Coat the parchment with coconut oil. 2. In a large bowl, stir together the ¼ cup of melted coconut oil, erythritol, and stevia powder. 3. Beat in the egg and vanilla. 4. Add the almond flour, baking powder, and sea salt and beat until well combined. 5. Gently fold in the chocolate and walnuts. 6. Transfer the dough to the prepared insert and press it into an even layer, covering the bottom of the insert. Cover and cook for 2½ hours on low. Using the parchment as a sling, lift the cookie out of the insert and transfer to a wire rack to cool. Cut into squares and serve warm or at room temperature.

Quick Chocolate Walnut Fudge

Prep Time: 15 minutes | Cook Time: 2 hours | Serves: 12

Coconut oil, for coating the slow cooker insert and a baking dish
1 cup canned coconut milk
4 ounces unsweetened chocolate, chopped
1 cup erythritol

2 teaspoons stevia powder
¼ teaspoon fine sea salt
2 teaspoons pure vanilla extract
1 cup chopped toasted walnuts

1. Generously coat the inside of the slow cooker insert with coconut oil. 2. Whisk the coconut milk into a uniform consistency in a large bowl. Add the chocolate, erythritol, stevia powder, and sea salt. Stir to mix well. Pour into the slow cooker. Cover and cook for 2 hours on low. 3. When finished, stir in the vanilla. 4. Let the fudge sit in the slow cooker, with the lid off, until it cools to room temperature, about 3 hours. 5. Coat a large baking dish with coconut oil and set aside. 6. Stir the fudge until it becomes glossy, about 10 minutes. 7. Stir in the walnuts. Transfer the mixture to the prepared baking dish and smooth it into an even layer with a rubber spatula. Refrigerate overnight. Serve chilled, cut into small pieces.

Fresh Berry Cobbler

Prep Time: 10 minutes | Cook Time: 2 hours | Serves: 8

4 cups mixed fresh berries
2½ tablespoons brown sugar
3 tablespoons minced fresh mint
1 cup flour
1½ tablespoons sugar

½ teaspoon ground ginger
1 egg
¼ cup evaporated milk (regular or low-fat)
1½ tablespoons vegetable oil
Cooking spray

1. Toss the berries, brown sugar, and mint in a large bowl. Set aside. 2. Combine the dry ingredients in a medium bowl. Beat in the egg, evaporated milk, and oil until a thick dough forms. 3. Spray a 4-quart slow cooker with cooking spray. Spread the dough along the bottom, taking care to cover the entire bottom with no gaps. Add the berries in an even layer. 4. Cook on low for 2 hours. 5. When finished, serve.

Sweet Pineapple Upside-Down Cake

Prep Time: 10 minutes | Cook Time: 4 hours | Serves: 8

1 (18-ounce) box yellow or butter cake mix
Cooking spray
¼ cup butter, melted

2 packed tablespoons brown sugar
1 (15-ounce) can crushed pineapple, undrained
Maraschino cherries (optional)

1. Make the cake mix according to the package directions. 2. Treat the bottom and sides of a 4-quart slow cooker with cooking spray. 3. Pour the butter into the slow cooker, lifting and tilting the crock to evenly coat the bottom. Evenly sprinkle the brown sugar on top of the butter. Carefully spoon the crushed pineapple over the brown sugar, and then pour in any juice remaining in the can. If using, cut the maraschino cherries in half and arrange as many as you want, cut side up, over the pineapple. 4. Carefully pour (or ladle) the prepared cake batter over the mixture on the bottom of the slow cooker. Cover and cook on low for 4 hours or until a toothpick inserted into the cake comes out clean. If the cake is too moist on top, remove the cover and cook for another 15–30 minutes. Allow to cool and then serve.

Delicious Strawberry Pandowdy

Prep Time: 10 minutes | Cook Time: 1 ½ hours | Serves: 4

4 cups whole strawberries, stems removed
½ teaspoon ground ginger
1½ tablespoons sugar
½ teaspoon cornstarch

¾ cup flour
3 tablespoons cold unsalted butter, cubed
3 tablespoons cold water
⅛ teaspoon table salt

1. Place the strawberries, ginger, sugar, and cornstarch into a 2-quart slow cooker. Toss to distribute evenly. 2. Place the flour, butter, water, and salt into a food processor. Mix until a solid ball of dough forms. Roll it out on a clean surface until it is about ¼"–½" thick and will completely cover the fruit in the insert. 3. Drape the dough over the strawberries. Cover and cook on high for 40 minutes. Remove the lid. Using the tip of a knife, cut the dough into 2-inch squares while still in the slow cooker. Keep the lid off and continue to cook on high for an additional 40 minutes. Serve hot.

Summer Blueberry Slump with Dumplings

Prep Time: 10 minutes | Cook Time: 2 hours | Serves: 8

4 cups fresh blueberries
1½ tablespoons sugar
1 teaspoon minced fresh ginger
1 cup flour
½ teaspoon ground ginger

1 egg
¼ cup evaporated milk, regular or low-fat
1½ tablespoons canola oil
Cooking spray

1. Toss the berries, sugar, and fresh ginger together in a large bowl. Set aside. 2. Whisk the flour and ground ginger in a medium bowl. Beat in the egg, evaporated milk, and canola oil until a thick dough forms. Shape into 2 dumplings. 3. Spray the inside of a 4-quart slow cooker with cooking spray. Add the berries in an even layer. Drop in the dumplings. 4. Cook on low for 2 hours. 5. When finished, serve.

Lucky Chai Tapioca Pudding

Prep Time: 10 minutes | Cook Time: 2 hours | Serves: 6

2 chai tea bags
2 cups evaporated milk (low-fat or fat-free)
⅓ packed cup brown sugar
½ teaspoon ground cinnamon
½ teaspoon ground star anise

½ teaspoon mace
½ teaspoon ground cardamom
¼ cup small pearl tapioca
1 egg

1. Steep the tea bags in the evaporated milk for 20 minutes. Discard the bags. Whisk in the sugar, spices, and tapioca. 2. Pour the mixture into a 2- or 4-quart slow cooker and cook on low heat for 1½ hours. Stir in the egg and continue to cook for 30 minutes. 3. When finished, serve.

Walnut Banana Bread

Prep Time: 15 minutes | Cook Time: 2-3 hours | Serves: 8

Cooking spray
2 cups all-purpose flour
1 cup granulated sugar
¼ teaspoon baking soda
2 teaspoons baking powder
½ teaspoon table salt

3 medium ripe bananas, mashed
6 tablespoons unsalted butter, softened
2 large eggs, beaten
¼ cup plain yogurt
1 teaspoon vanilla extract
1¼ cups walnuts

1. Spray the inside of a 4-quart slow cooker with the cooking spray. 2. Whisk together the flour, sugar, baking powder, baking soda, and salt in a medium-sized mixing bowl. Set aside. 3. In a food processor, add the bananas, butter, eggs, yogurt, and vanilla. Pulse to cream together. 4. Add the walnuts and flour mixture to the food processor. Pulse to combine and to chop the walnuts. Scrape down the sides of the container with a spatula; continue to pulse until mixed. 5. Add the batter to the prepared slow cooker and use a spatula to spread it evenly across the bottom of the crock. 6. Cover and cook on high for 2–3 hours, or until a toothpick inserted in the center of the bread comes out clean. 7. Allow to cool uncovered before removing it from the slow cooker.

Sweet Ginger Poached Pears

Prep Time: 5 minutes | Cook Time: 4 hours | Serves: 8

5 pears, peeled, cored, and cut into wedges
3 cups water
1 cup white granulated sugar

2 tablespoons ginger, minced
1 teaspoon cinnamon

1. Add all ingredients to a 4-quart slow cooker. Cover and cook on low heat for 4 hours. 2. When finished, serve.

Chocolate Chip Brownies

Prep Time: 10 minutes | Cook Time: 4-6 hours | Serves: 9

Cooking spray
¾ cup almond flour
¼ cup plus 2 tablespoons powdered erythritol sweetener of your choice
¼ cup unsweetened cocoa powder
½ teaspoon baking powder

4 large eggs
4 ounces low-fat cream cheese, softened
6 tablespoons unsalted butter, melted
1½ teaspoons vanilla extract
½ cup chocolate chips

1. Coat a slow cooker generously with cooking spray. 2. In a small bowl, mix together the almond flour, erythritol, cocoa powder, and baking powder and set aside. 3. In a large bowl, mix together the eggs, cream cheese, butter, and vanilla. Slowly stir in the almond flour mixture and mix to combine. Stir in the chocolate chips. 4. Pour the batter into the slow cooker. 5. Place a paper towel between the slow cooker and the lid to cut down on any condensation that develops. Cook on low for 4 to 6 hours or on high for 2 to 3 hours, or until a toothpick inserted in the center comes out clean.

Homemade Strawberry Cobbler

Prep Time: 15 minutes | Cook Time: 4-6 hours | Serves: 8

Cooking spray
2 cups fresh strawberries
3 tablespoons powdered erythritol sweetener of your choice, divided
1 large egg

½ cup coconut oil
1 teaspoon vanilla
1 cup coconut flour
1 cup almond flour

1. Coat a slow cooker generously with cooking spray. 2. Place the berries on the bottom of the slow cooker and sprinkle them with 2 tablespoons of erythritol. 3. In a large bowl, mix together the egg, coconut oil, remaining 1 tablespoon erythritol, and the vanilla. Fold in the coconut flour and the almond flour, mixing well until a thick batter forms. 4. Spread the batter evenly on top of the berries with the back of a spoon or your hand and press it down lightly. 5. Place a paper towel between the slow cooker and the lid to cut down on any condensation that develops. Cook on low for 4 to 6 hours or on high for 2 to 3 hours, or until a toothpick inserted in the center comes out clean.

Traditional Winter Gingerbread

Prep Time: 10 minutes | Cook Time: 3 hours | Serves: 12

Cooking spray
2 cups almond flour
¾ cup powdered erythritol sweetener of your choice
2 tablespoons coconut flour
2 tablespoons ground ginger
2 teaspoons baking powder
2 teaspoons ground cinnamon

½ teaspoon ground nutmeg
¼ teaspoon ground cloves
Pinch salt
¾ cup heavy (whipping) cream
½ cup butter, melted
4 eggs
1 teaspoon pure vanilla extract

1. Coat a slow cooker generously with cooking spray. 2. In a large bowl, stir together the erythritol, coconut flour, almond flour, ginger, baking powder, cinnamon, nutmeg, cloves, and salt. 3. In a medium bowl, whisk together the cream, butter, eggs, and vanilla. 4. Add the wet ingredients to the dry ingredients and stir to combine. 5. Spoon the batter into the insert. 6. Cover and cook on low for 3 hours, or until a toothpick inserted in the center comes out clean. 7. Serve warm.

Conclusion

The Crock Pot is more than just a kitchen appliance—it's a game-changer for anyone seeking convenience, flavor, and nourishment in their meals. With its ability to transform simple ingredients into tender, delicious dishes, it has earned its placc as a staple in households around the world. From hearty stews to flavorful roasts, the Crock Pot makes cooking accessible, enjoyable, and stress-free, allowing you to focus on what matters most—spending time with loved ones or simply unwinding after a busy day.

The Ultimate Crock Pot Cookbook for Beginners takes this experience to the next level by providing a curated collection of recipes tailored for all skill levels. Whether you're a busy professional, a parent juggling multiple responsibilities, or someone new to cooking, this cookbook has been thoughtfully designed to cater to your needs. Each recipe offers clear instructions, time-saving tips, and a variety of flavors to suit any occasion.

With its focus on practicality and variety, the cookbook ensures you'll never run out of inspiration. From comforting soups to delectable desserts, the recipes are not only easy to follow but also highlight the Crock Pot's versatility. Imagine coming home to the aroma of a slow-cooked meal or impressing guests with effortless culinary creations—this cookbook makes it all possible.

Ultimately, the Crock Pot and its companion cookbook empower you to embrace the art of slow cooking with ease. Whether you're preparing a quick weeknight dinner or a festive feast, this duo is your key to achieving delicious results every time. Dive in, get cooking, and discover the joy of crafting meals that bring comfort, flavor, and a touch of magic to your table.

Appendix 1 Measurement Conversion Chart

VOLUME EQUIVALENTS (LIQUID)

US STANDARD	US STANDARD (OUNCES)	METRIC (APPROXIMATE)
2 tablespoons	1 fl.oz	30 mL
¼ cup	2 fl.oz	60 mL
½ cup	4 fl.oz	120 mL
1 cup	8 fl.oz	240 mL
1½ cup	12 fl.oz	355 mL
2 cups or 1 pint	16 fl.oz	475 mL
4 cups or 1 quart	32 fl.oz	1 L
1 gallon	128 fl.oz	4 L

VOLUME EQUIVALENTS (DRY)

US STANDARD	METRIC (APPROXIMATE)
⅛ teaspoon	0.5 mL
¼ teaspoon	1 mL
½ teaspoon	2 mL
¾ teaspoon	4 mL
1 teaspoon	5 mL
1 tablespoon	15 mL
¼ cup	59 mL
½ cup	118 mL
¾ cup	177 mL
1 cup	235 mL
2 cups	475 mL
3 cups	700 mL
4 cups	1 L

TEMPERATURES EQUIVALENTS

FAHRENHEIT (F)	CELSIUS (C) (APPROXIMATE)
225°F	107°C
250°F	120°C
275°F	135°C
300°F	150°C
325°F	160°C
350°F	180°C
375°F	190°C
400°F	205°C
425°F	220°C
450°F	235°C
475°F	245°C
500°F	260°C

WEIGHT EQUIVALENTS

US STANDARD	METRIC (APPROXINATE)
1 ounce	28 g
2 ounces	57 g
5 ounces	142 g
10 ounces	284 g
15 ounces	425g
16 ounces (1 pound)	455 g
1.5pounds	680 g
2pounds	907g

Appendix 2 Recipes Index

Made in United States
Troutdale, OR
01/11/2025

27844054R00065